Why wasn't I taught this

"What a wonderful book! I already want to read it again........ There are so many tips and pointers that I will take with me and dip back into the book if ever I'm lacking motivation. I feel so fortunate to have all this life knowledge at my fingertips so early on in my career, all in one handy book! Thank you very much for writing it." **Alice Smith**

"This book is the best book I have ever read on what is necessary to create a successful life for yourself..... this book illustrates how to be really happy and successful...... And I do believe that reading this book will also highlight the fact that everyone has skills and abilities that they might not think they have.....Definitely recommend that you should get this book and read it. It will help you work out what you really want from life, and provide you with an approach to get there."
Dave the Engineer 'Engineer Critic'

"David Reynolds' book is full of practical, down-to-earth advice based on a wealth of real experience at the sharp end of business. He covers everything from time-structuring, to prioritising......shared in a concise, accessible way, that make each nugget easy to digest and apply..... His style is straightforward, like having a highly successful favourite uncle as your personal coach. Read this book - you'll keep coming back to it again and again for its good advice." **Susan Courtney**

"Only read this book if you're dedicated to increasing your (and other people's) store of wealth, health and happiness!" **James Hardiman**

"I have just finished the book and it has been an absolute joy... I feel back on track, energised, motivated and excited about my life and what is possible.

This guide is simply written and laid out, there's no jargon, no hype - just fantastic and inspiring content based on genuine experience..... I felt like I was in conversation with David, it was fantastic being led, step-by-step.

This book is amazing... whether you are looking for an inspiration, a reminder of what can be achieved, a confidence boost or a life changing read, then you really should buy this book and discover for yourself the secrets of the rich and successful." **Leesa Daymond**

To Callie
With best wishes

Why wasn't I taught this at school?

How to get the most out of life and other useful stuff

Dave Reynolds

Published by New Generation Publishing in 2013

Copyright © David Reynolds 2013

First Edition

The author asserts the moral right under the Copyright, Designs and Patents Act 1988 to be identified as the author of this work.

All Rights reserved. No part of this publication may be reproduced, stored in a retrieval system or transmitted, in any form or by any means without the prior consent of the author, nor be otherwise circulated in any form of binding or cover other than that which it is published and without a similar condition being imposed on the subsequent purchaser.

www.newgeneration-publishing.com

New Generation **Publishing**

Foreword

Since my book 'Power Secrets of the Rich and Successful' was first published in the spring of 2009 the economic landscape has continued to show little sign of a sustained recovery.

The Eurozone is looking ever more fragile, unemployment rates, especially those of young people, are of concern, the housing market remains stubbornly sluggish and pension prospects for the majority of the working population are looking increasingly bleak.

The cost of studying for a University Degree, and the obstacles facing 'first time buyers' in obtaining mortgages, has resulted in the outlook for young people being decidedly more challenging than it was for several previous generations.

This scenario has prompted me to revisit some of the text and the focus of the earlier edition of my book in order to address these issues, as best I can, especially for those starting out in adult life.

Particularly as, in my opinion, there are so many lessons of paramount importance which we fail to teach in our schools.

The principles and techniques I shared in the original version are timeless. They worked when I was young, are still relevant several decades later, and will continue to remain so. However I have added new material aimed at people in their late teens and early twenties. This is the age before erroneous, and possibly harmful, patterns of thought and behaviour become too deeply entrenched. So there is an extra chapter at the end of this edition specifically for those who are still in their twenties.

This is the age that so many people refer back to much later in life and say, "If only I had known then what I know now"

As far as I can tell most of the people who bought and read 'Power Secrets of the Rich and Successful' were aged between thirty and fifty and I have been thrilled and delighted by the wonderful testimonials I've received. Many told me however that they wished they had read a similar book when they were in their twenties.

By deliberately targeting a younger audience I want to make whatever contribution I can to the lives of an even larger number of people. Especially those who will eventually be responsible for shaping the future for the next and future generations.

Which is why I have changed the title.

The majority of the text from the original book remains the same, but I have revised, added to and updated some of the sections to reflect the challenges and opportunities that confront us today. There are plenty of both.

Furthermore I have addressed, in more detail, issues facing those in the midpoint of working life who may be feeling decidedly uneasy about their financial situation in retirement.

Universal Principles don't ever change. Only the way they are applied may require a little adaptation according to the times in which we live.

INTRODUCTION

This is a book about achieving success in your life and living up to your true potential.

Right now you may not know exactly how you would define success as far as you are concerned and it's probable that you may severely underestimate your potential.

But by the time you have reached the end of this book you will have a much clearer idea of many things you want to achieve, and a much more positive and accurate belief in your ability to do so.

For some people the acquisition of wealth is a major priority. Others may have very different ambitions. Whatever your aspirations might be you are about to take a quantum leap towards ensuring your dreams become reality.

This is not a 'get rich quick' book, but between us we can make you rich if that's one of your goals. We can certainly make you more successful in a multitude of other ways too.

It won't happen overnight but it will happen. From the moment you start applying the principles I'm about to share you will feel a surge of energy. You'll quickly become more confident, more self directed and full of expectation.

I initially retired in 1999 when I was fifty-eight and was in the fortunate position of being financially independent.
    However it soon became apparent that having little or nothing to do most days wasn't all it's cracked up to be.
    Being idle for long spells doesn't appeal to me.
    To keep myself occupied I accepted offers to work with various companies on a consultancy basis. Let me tell you, it's much more fun to work when you don't have to!

During the years since I first retired my net worth has probably tripled. You'll understand how this can happen when you get to the sections which deal with **Money** and **Wealth**. But don't be tempted to jump ahead. It's important that you read all the preceding pages first.

The reason for telling you this is to make clear that writing and marketing this book is not about making money for me, it's about making money for you. It's not about making me a success, it's about you achieving success.

I've been sharing success principles with people who I have worked with, over a long period of time. It's because so many of them urged me to put it all into the form of a book that I eventually decided to do so.

What I want to share with you will fast track you to success in all your endeavours. Furthermore it will promote your good health, and lead you to enjoy a rich, happy and fulfilling life.

But there is a price to pay. You will have to apply the principles that you are about to encounter. No more putting things off.
    There is no 'free lunch'.

Although we don't know each other I want you to read this book as if I am your personal friend, speaking to you and you alone. I'm going to be candid with you, and you will need to be honest with yourself. Let's work together to make you happier, wealthier and far more successful than you are right now.

Are you ready?

Part One

Your Journey Starts Here

Chapter One

Get Prepared to Succeed

Everybody is 'self-made', but only the successful are prepared to admit it!

Do you want to live your life to the full?

Do you want to live up to your true potential?

Do you want more money than you have now and to be free of debt?

Do you want many of the things that money can buy?

Do you want to improve your relationships?

Do you want the esteem and respect of others?

Do you have dreams that you want to become reality?

Then come with me on this journey where you will discover the keys that can give you everything you want from your life.

I can promise you that this book can change your life and will show you how to enjoy an abundance of wealth, good health, and great happiness.

It doesn't matter where you started from or where you are now. It makes no difference.

You can achieve virtually everything you could wish for by simply adopting the strategies which are about to be shared with you.

I am living proof of the impact these universal principles are going to have on your life!

For reasons I'm about to explain, when I was in my early twenties I developed the habit of observing people who excel at what they do, because I wanted to learn their secret.
Over the years I've had the good fortune to encounter a great number of

successful and wealthy individuals. Many of them I now consider as close friends or associates. They've taught me some valuable lessons.

But let me start from the beginning.
I was born into a typical working class family. My father was a lorry driver and my mother worked part-time at a Co-op grocers.
Nobody on either side of my family had ever gone to University so, although I achieved reasonably good exam results at age sixteen ('O' Levels), it never appealed or occurred to me to continue my formal education.
Many of the friends I had at the time were somewhat older than me, and were already at work and earning money, and I couldn't wait to do the same.

My first job, from leaving school, was as a laboratory assistant in a large Pharmaceutical Company. It was a condition of employment that I attended night classes, as well as college for one day a week, in order to study for the 'A' Levels that I would have taken had I stayed in full time education.

It wasn't for me.
It didn't take long before I realised I was the wrong person in the wrong job.

But at the weekends I had a Saturday job, working on a mobile greengrocery van, and had been able to save enough money to fix up my father's car. It was a very old Morris Ten which hadn't been out of our garage for several years because sadly my Dad could no longer afford to run it.

Soon after my seventeenth birthday I passed my driving test and began driving to work. On the way I often spotted my boss waiting at his bus stop, so I would stop to give him a lift.
That was when I knew for certain I was in the wrong job! If he was my boss, but unable to afford his own car, how was I ever going to become rich doing the same job as him?

Eventually I gave up my illustrious career as a laboratory assistant, much to the disappointment of my mother and father, and set out to earn my fortune as a commission only Vacuum Cleaner salesman.....which was the only sales job I could get at 18 years of age.
Not really the best job in the world, but looking back now I realise it

was to play a big part in teaching me the importance of overcoming inertia and fear.

But more of that later....

After about ten months of 'cold calling' and knocking on the doors of some of the biggest houses I'd ever seen (my knees were often knocking louder than the door-knocker was) my uncle got me a salaried job in the furniture department of a large Department Store.

At least the hours were more civilised and I was working indoors!

However, after about four years there, I again looked for a way to earn more money as although I enjoyed selling furniture, carpets and electrical goods; a career in retail was not particularly well paid.

By the time I reached my early twenties, I again became a 'commission only' salesman, this time selling Personal Accident Insurance. I'd been enticed by the promise that I could earn a big income.

But 'commission only' means if you don't make any sales you don't make any money. You only get paid on results.

During my first year in the job I sold quite a lot. My camera...my stereo...my car...!

Just kidding!

But in reality that's not too far from the truth. I was certainly not making enough money to pay all the bills.

Gradually I discovered what it was like to be absolutely broke and falling deeper and deeper in debt.

This wouldn't have been so serious but for the fact I was now married with a wife and baby son to support, with another baby on the way. We had bought a large house which, at the time, was considerably beyond what we could afford. Needless to say, I had taken on a big mortgage, having implied to the Building Society that I was earning more than I really was.

All this was a long time ago now, but I still vividly remember the sleepless nights, the cold sweats, and the desperate feelings of panic as the debts mounted up.

Looking back I'll be forever grateful to my manager at the time, Stanley Browne.

When I was at my lowest point he took the trouble to drive over a hundred miles from his home in order to sit down with me and help me sort out the mess I'd got myself in.

He didn't give me money. He gave me something which turned out to be much more valuable. He gave me encouragement and good advice. He made me face up to my situation and work out exactly what condition my financial affairs were in.

Above all, he gave me the courage to start battling my way out of the serious amount of debt that I'd allowed to build up.

As a result of that meeting I became determined not to have to sell the house of which I was so proud, and that 'if some people could earn high incomes, so could I'.

The alternative would have been to throw in the towel and admit humiliating defeat.

The lessons I learned during that period of my life have since enabled me to achieve things which, at the time, would have been beyond my wildest dreams.

That's when and why I became so eager to learn what it was that separated the winners in life from the 'also-rans'.

Amongst the people that have influenced me in my life was W.Clement Stone. He was the Founder and Chairman of the American owned Insurance Company I was working for.

I met him many times and got to know him well.

He was a passionate believer in the importance of positive thinking and was the co-author with Napoleon Hill of the book 'Success through a Positive Mental Attitude'.

Previously Napoleon Hill had authored a book which is still regarded by many today as the greatest self-help book ever written. The book is entitled 'Think and Grow Rich' and has been responsible for thousands of its readers becoming multi-millionaires.

Certainly I know that I benefitted enormously from being exposed to some of these success principles so early in my life. This is what has motivated me to share with you what I've learned.

Since those days, I have continually endeavoured to recognise the qualities, and the strategies of people who consistently demonstrate the ability to succeed.

The one thing that quickly became obvious is that, regardless of whether these 'high-flyers' chosen field is business, sports, the arts, or one of the professions…, the similarities between them are far greater than the differences. I recognised with undeniable clarity that they all share several common traits. They employ and practice the same habits; they demonstrate many common qualities, and display remarkably similar attitudes.

As a result of my abiding interest about 'what makes winners tick' several years ago I began to document a list of the principles which I considered critical to getting the most out of myself – and eventually as a business executive, getting the best out of others also.

So I have gradually developed an account of what has evolved to become my own philosophy - unashamedly learned from scores of 'high-flyers' whose success I have admired and tried to emulate.

I'll be forever grateful to all the individuals who have had a profound and lasting effect upon me.

I have a lifestyle that allows me to do pretty much whatever I want, whenever I want.

At the end of 2007 I again decided to ease back from working full time. I have had a fulfilling, varied and long career, and have accumulated far more wealth than I could have ever imagined possible when I was that young laboratory assistant!

Our children have grown up and left home. My wife and I are able to travel regularly and take long trips. We can also spend more time with our friends and family. We intend to continue enjoying life to the full.

Now please don't think that I'm on some 'ego trip' trying to impress you. I simply want to establish my credentials. Frankly I'm not 'super rich' in the way that a Richard Branson or a Philip Green are, and I haven't been invited to join the panel of 'The Dragons Den', but I have become financially independent, and I can teach you to do likewise.

So how did I get from where I was, when I was totally broke, to where I am now? Free to do whatever I wish, live how I want to live, drive the cars I want to drive and travel to the places I want to see?

And more important, as far as you are concerned, *how can you do the same?*

This is why I'm going to share with you a powerful, practical, and exceedingly effective system, which I guarantee will put you on the road to achieving the very most from your life.

You are only going to pass this way once. You're not in rehearsal.

The following information will change your life for the better and forever!

If you want to live a great life – and who doesn't? –then you'd better start doing something about it right now.

Because your life won't change unless you do!

There are no barriers to success - only those that you've imposed upon yourself or allowed others to impose on you.

You are going to learn how to break through those barriers. Put into practice what you will discover in these pages and I know beyond any doubt that you will transform your life.

I don't care who you are or what you are. It's of no consequence as to how old you are, or how young you are. What sex you are, or what your background is, doesn't matter one iota.

The very fact that you are reading this is sufficient proof that you have within you the desire to do better, and become better, than you currently are.

I'm going to show you how!

By reading this book as if I was talking directly and solely to you, you can regard me as your personal mentor.

All you need is an open mind and an honest and sincere desire to succeed in making your dreams come true. *And to stop making excuses for yourself!*

This book is dedicated to enabling you to become a more positive, focused and happier person. It will do wonders for your self-esteem. You will find your self-image will improve day after day, week after week and bring you closer and closer to becoming the success you really want to be.

If it's tangible wealth that you want, the secrets to making more money than you may think possible, are going to be revealed to you.

Reading this book and employing the principles it contains is going to change your life. You can bank on it!

You won't change overnight…but you will change. The process may start slowly at first but will rapidly accelerate. You are about to begin fulfilling your potential...

Now consider the following statement very carefully because it's absolutely true:

However you see yourself at the moment has a tremendous impact on how you currently think, act and behave.

There is no escaping this fact. It's true for all of us.

But you are going to gradually change the way you see yourself!

Don't be concerned if you don't fully understand the significance of the above statement.
   Very soon we are going to explore it in much greater detail.

It took a 'eureka moment' for me to recognise how this single vital incontrovertible fact would enable me to take total control of my own life, and would provide the key to inspiring many others to achieve wealth and success in their lives too.
   Follow the concepts and adopt the powerful philosophies I'm sharing with you, and you'll begin to act differently. When you act differently you'll begin to think differently.
   You'll acquire success habits and discard harmful habits.
   Your confidence will grow and your personal expectations and aspirations will soar!

There's a whole variety of ways to define success, and each of us may define it differently as far as ourselves, as individuals, is concerned; but almost everybody wants to achieve success in some way or another.

   Success in your career or your business.
   Success in your relationships.
   Success as a parent.
   Success in sport.
   Acquiring wealth. *(Money may not be everything, but for many of us it's right up there with oxygen as Zig Ziglar used to say!)*
   Enjoying good health.
   Contributing to society.

There are so many areas in which we can strive to achieve things and measure ourselves. Success in any endeavour owes little or nothing to age, appearance, sex, colour, background, education or nationality. Look around you. There's no way neither you nor I can lay the blame on our upbringing or background for failing to accomplish anything worthwhile in our lives. Admittedly some people start with huge advantages, but many of those same people squander their advantages. Equally, thousands who never had much of a start in life achieve great things.

So what really does make the difference? Why is it that some people lead such happy and fulfilling lives whilst the majority seem to be permanently struggling? Why do some people seem to attract good fortune when many seem to stagger from one crisis to the next?

What makes some people fight on when others give up?

How is it that some people are a pleasure to be with – whilst others can brighten up a room just by leaving?

What causes some people to constantly get sick when others hardly ever suffer even a mild cold?

How come some people have allowed themselves to get horribly overweight when others enjoy staying in good shape?

Why do we find some people fascinating and engaging when others bore us to tears?

How is it that some people seem to have masses of energy when others are always tired?

What reason could there be that some people do their best work under pressure, when others complain of being stressed out?

If you are looking for the answers to some of these questions and you want to get more out of your life, please consider this book to have been written especially for you.

Additionally, if you are responsible for managing or supervising others, or intend to do so at some time in the future, then reading and practising what I'm sharing with you will improve their performances as well as your own.

It's all down to the way you think. The way you act. And what you say to yourself. The internal dialogue that continually goes on in your head.

The practices and the proven techniques you'll encounter here are what I've learned through years of observing many high achievers it has been my good fortune to have known and, in some cases, worked with. It is a compendium of 'best practices'.

They will change the way you see yourself. They will help you think like a high achiever. And when you learn to think like one you are going to act like one. And when you start to act like one you are on the way to becoming one!

You are going to achieve things in your life that right now may seem impossible.

No two people are exactly the same. Each of us has a unique personality and character. Some of it inherited. But most of it learned.

Our habits of both thoughts and actions have been acquired. We weren't born with them!

What I'm seeking to do, is to help you set exciting and worthwhile goals, point you in their direction, and show you how to achieve them. This book is written in a way you can dip into easily and regularly, but you must read it in its entirety first.

Before proceeding any further, you will obtain the maximum benefit by taking a few minutes right now to think about what you really want to achieve in your life; even if you only look a few years ahead.

We'll be going to go into much more depth on how to set and achieve goals later, but it's important for you to immediately begin adopting a 'success focused' frame of mind.

Imagine seeing yourself as you'd like to be in, let's say, five years from now.

What job or business might you be in? What type of car will you be driving?

What kind of house are you going to be living in?

What will you have achieved during those five years?

Please get a clean sheet of paper and write down some of the things you would dearly love to achieve in your life.

You don't have to define everything in too much detail at this point. You may not even know what career path you want to follow. That doesn't matter. Even though we will address the specific process of goal setting later, it's important that you start to think now about what you really want.

If you don't know where you are going how will you ever get anywhere?

So what are some of those dreams and ambitions? Before you go any further I urge you to write out a list.

Why are you reading this anyway? You surely hope that it might help you accomplish something. So what is that something and when do you want to accomplish it by?

Write down at least one major objective. More if you can. Be as specific as possible. Put it on a card or a piece of paper and keep it handy and where you can easily access it. Don't show it to anybody else.

You don't have to try to change the world. ***But just think what you might attempt if you were confident that you would succeed.***

Writing your goals down will make you far better equipped and much more likely to achieve them. Don't worry if your ambitions are not mind-boggling. That can come later. You will soon feel confident in setting many more goals – and even higher ones!

Most people go through their entire lives with no clear idea of what they would really like to do. So don't be surprised if at the moment you can't be crystal clear about what you want to be or what you want to do for the next twenty or thirty years. Just look ahead a few years, and visualise what you would be thrilled to achieve.

Setting and achieving goals can be a bit like taking a boat out to sea and heading towards the horizon. The further you travel the further you can see. Make sure that the goal or goals you are setting – at least for now – are believable and achievable. We'll talk about achieving 'impossible dreams' as we continue to make progress.

Now this isn't only about achieving material goals. It's also about being happier. Becoming more confident. Enjoying better relationships. Having more energy. Enjoying good health.

In other words, living life to the full!

These are proven powerful universal principles that will enable you to live up to your full potential. Regardless of who you are, what you are, and where you are today!

Together we are going to make sure you adopt a way of thinking and behaviour that will bring you an abundance of happiness and fulfilment. Very soon you will be able to positively affect others around you as you grow in confidence and ability.

My mission is all about enabling you to get the most out of yourself and your own life. We are also going to recognise however, that in order to turn your dreams into reality it's going to be necessary to tap into the assistance and endeavours of other people. So you are going to discover a host of ways in which you can inspire and encourage others to achieve great things also.

But first you must start with yourself!

Chapter Two

Your Greatest Power

Compared to many millions of people living in third world countries you already live a privileged existence. Nevertheless it's probable that you are falling far short of how you would really like to live in today's affluent western society.

My guess is that if you are like a lot of people in the United Kingdom, you feel frustrated with several aspects of your current lifestyle. After all, if you were totally satisfied with your life as it currently is today, it's most unlikely that you would be reading this.

We have to acknowledge that, in life, there are some things we cannot change....our notorious British weather for example, and some of the breathtakingly incompetent decisions of our politicians and cabinet ministers. But within the framework of things we may not be able to easily change, the one thing we can do is to change ourselves and the way we live!

What may have been acceptable to our great grandparents is certainly not the way most of us want to live today.
    With the world so accessible, many of us want to visit exciting and exotic places, travelling in comfort and staying in luxurious hotels.

Owning a desirable home, and driving the car of your choice, may feature high on your 'wish list'.
    Eating out in decent restaurants and savouring a bottle of good wine is something you may want to regularly enjoy. Owning a wardrobe full of nice clothes might well have some appeal too.
    So if you aren't able to do all the things you would like to, but wish that you could, you have to ask yourself 'why not?'
    If you are occasionally indulging in some of these things, are you building up credit card debts by doing so?

Today we are living in a divided world.
    Having travelled to India, China and Africa, as well as Cambodia, Vietnam, Indonesia and the Philippines over the last few years, I've seen some appalling poverty at first hand on a huge scale.

Today unfortunately we also have a divided society right here on our own doorstep; and it will get worse.

The scale of household debt on credit cards, mortgages, personal loans and overdrafts is greater than ever. Not all debt is bad of course, as will be explained in detail later, but too many people are in danger of sinking in a sea of debt from which they are unlikely to ever escape.

What makes matters even worse is the situation we have reached where most pension schemes, whether company or private, will no longer provide sufficient benefits for a comfortable retirement. Fewer people than ever are even in a worthwhile pension scheme.

We have an ageing population, who are living longer, but the ratio of people working and paying National Insurance compared to the number of people receiving state pensions is rapidly reducing. This is a recipe for potential disaster!

To put this into perspective, during the tax year 2012/2013 weekly state pension for a married couple was £171.85. If there was no other household income Pension credits may have increased it to £236.79 a week.

Very soon the system will be simplified and there is to be one rate for everybody. This will start at around £144 per week but will rise annually in line with inflation. However the age at which you will become eligible for this is going to gradually increase. You may well be seventy before receiving it!

Can you imagine what life is going to be be like for two people having to exist on such a meagre income?

So what will the future hold for you, as you get to retirement age?
Are you going to be amongst the one percent who will be very wealthy and totally financially independent? Or perhaps you will be among the fortunate four percent who will retire comfortably without the need to adjust their lifestyle?

Or are you heading in the direction of the ninety-five percent who will be forced to cut down on doing many of the things they used to enjoy, possibly having to endure a life bordering on abject poverty. How awful to have to choose between eating properly or keeping warm.
Do you really want to rely upon your kids to help support you? What guarantee do you have that they will even be able to?

Don't put your head in the sand and try to pretend this problem doesn't exist.

Whatever your age at the moment, barring an unforeseen tragedy, you are one day going to reach the point where you will either want to, or have to, stop working, and your regular income will cease.

So what's your plan? Will you have accumulated enough money to ensure you can live well and free from worry and financial anxiety?

If this is giving you some cause for concern then it's time for you to face up to reality, and decide now to change course. You *can* do it.

You may well be saying right now that it's too difficult to think about planning for retirement as you have much more pressing needs to deal with today.

So let's step back from the future and look at your position as it is right now.

And now you'd better really pay attention, because what I'm about to tell you is one of the most important things I've ever learned. *And it's the key to your future prosperity.*

You are where you are today because of all the choices you've made in your life up till now.

In other words, if you are not happy with the way things are at the moment, you've only yourself to blame! The only exception being those who may have been born with a major disability, or have been seriously injured in an accident for which they were not to blame, or suffering from a disabling disease.

Your choices and decisions have brought you to where you are now. I know that sounds harsh, but you'd better believe it and accept it.

By way of illustration I'll give some examples:-

On average people in the UK *choose* to watch 23 hours a week of television. That's about half of the number of hours they spend at work! Do you think that high achievers watch that much TV? I think not!

Obese people *choose* to eat unhealthy food and more food than they should. That's how they got fat!

Many people *choose* to spend several hours a week listening to their favourite music, either in their cars or on i-pods. Nothing wrong with that, I like music too. But some of that time could be spent learning a new language or skill for example. There are stacks of educational CD's and MP3 downloads available today.

It's common knowledge that many people join fitness centres and then *choose* to hardly ever show up!

It would be easy to go on and on but no doubt you get the picture.

So how many things have *you* started but *chose* to never get around to finishing? How many good resolutions have *you* made in the past but *chose* not to live up to?

How much money have *you chosen* to squander on things you didn't need? How much time have *you chosen* to waste?

These choices were made by *you*, you can't blame anyone else.

Your greatest power is the power to choose!

Undoubtedly up to this moment in your life you have almost certainly made some wrong choices. That's true for everybody to some degree.

There's no point in feeling regret or remorse however, because what's done is done. Probably there's little that you can do now to undo or reverse what's gone before.

Don't start beating yourself up or feeling sorry for yourself, there's nothing to gain by doing that. The important thing is to learn from mistakes you may have made and move on.

It may be of some comfort to learn that, to some degree, you actually couldn't help it!

Here's why.

The choices you have made in the past, and will continue to make in the future, will always be consistent with who you think you are!

You cannot consistently perform in a way that is inconsistent with the way you see yourself. (Dr. Joyce Brothers)

Now here is the most revealing statement of all.

You are who you think you are, and you will become what you

think you'll become!

The fact is that each of us has a mental image of ourselves. It's called our 'self image'

Your 'self image' has been built up as a result of many influences and events that you have experienced in your life to date. For example:

The family environment in which you were raised.

The school you went to.

The kids you played with.

The successes and failures you experienced, especially when young.

The things people told you about yourself.

The list could go on and on. So many things have affected your perception of yourself.

Your childhood undoubtably played a major role in shaping the person you are today.

Hopefully you are one of the lucky ones who benefitted from being raised in a loving and wholesome family environment. But you may not have been not so fortunate.

Whatever your experiences were as a child however, you have to recognise that as an adult you have to take total responsibility for yourself. Regardless of your upbringing and education, from now on you are going to take total control of how you think about yourself and how you behave.

There's nothing that I can do to change whatever happened to you as a child which may have influenced the way you currently think and behave. And neither can you. But that's now all in the past.

You're not a child any more. You're an adult now and you can choose what you think, choose how you behave and choose what you believe about yourself.

If you had a difficult upbringing, with little to encourage you, then I'm really sorry. I don't mean for one moment to make light of whatever you may have been through.

But the worst possible outcome would be for you to mentally and emotionally carry your early experiences and feelings into the rest of your life.

If you think I'm being harsh in saying this let me suggest you read the story of Paul Connolly.
He had the most horrendous childhood you could possibly imagine.

Abandoned by his mother and literally left out with the rubbish when two weeks old, he spent his entire childhood in care. During the time he spent in a home in East London he, and many of the other children there, suffered terrible abuse. Sexual, physical and mental. The perpetrators, who were supposedly looking after them, were unspeakably evil.
Some of the kids he shared this life with are now dead, having taken their own lives or as a result of drug addiction.
By the time he was old enough to leave the care home Paul was filled with a rage of unimaginable proportions. Unable to read or write he became violent in the extreme.
There was a time he seriously considered shooting dead those who had tormented him as a child.

Today Paul is a totally different person than the man who walked out of that home consumed by hatred, anger and frustration.

I don't want to tell too much of Paul's story as I really recommend that you get a copy of his book and read it for yourself, even though it's a very harrowing account. His book is called **'Against All Odds. The most Amazing True Life Story You'll Ever Read'**
Believe me, the title is not an exaggeration!

The book is available from Amazon and, of course, can be downloaded on to Kindle.

When I read Paul's book I started to feel guilty that perhaps I had previously been too dismissive of those whose background was profoundly different from my own.
Unless you've experienced something for yourself it's a mistake to assume you can understand what another person may have endured and been affected by.

Perhaps in certain circumstances there's a case to be made for counselling and therapy. Those who simply cannot let go of a deeply distressing past could well be advised to seek professional help.

But one thing is for sure. Paul Connolly has demonstrated that it is possible to overcome the most extreme of childhood horrors and become a positive, successful and socially responsible person.

Today he has developed a successful career as a personal fitness trainer with many well known celebrities among his clients. He's happily married with two young sons.

His story is so inspiring that I knew I wanted to meet him. I wasn't disappointed when I did.

It was a privilege to spend time with a man who couldn't even read or write until enrolling in a literacy class in his mid twenties, and now has achieved so much in turning his life around and becoming a very likeable, articulate and engaging personality.

So, if Paul Connolly can overcome the worst start in life imaginable, you too can do the same if your life got off to a rough start. You do not have to be a victim of the legacy of your younger years.

If you allow yourself to become a prisoner of the past you will never be free to ordain your future.

You have to to cast off any erroneous beliefs about what you may or may not be able to achieve.

Most people have a preconceived idea of where they 'fit' in society. These notions are generally indoctrinated at an early age. Most people go through life never changing this mental picture of themselves.

But that's just what it is – a picture. It doesn't have to represent reality.

The problem is that all of our decisions, choices and actions are consistent with our self image.

Well known evidence of this is the number of people who won huge sums from the lottery only to become broke again within a few years.

All the bad decisions they made about spending and investing wasn't 'bad luck' as they may try to rationalise; it was because subconsciously their actions were being driven by the need to get back to where they were comfortable.

Their circumstances had changed, but their perception of themselves hadn't!

Years ago there was a famous football pools winner, Viv Nicholson, who declared when she collected her winnings that she was going to "spend, spend and spend". Three years later she was broke and back to exactly where she was before.

More recently you may recall reading of a lottery winner who won three and a half million pounds only to wind up practically penniless just three years later. This is a guy who spent a fortune on expensive cars even though he couldn't even drive!

Mike Tyson reportedly earned over $400,000,000!! How much has he got now?
    None of it!
    It's impossible to over emphasise how important it is to understand and accept that all our thoughts and actions are consistent with our self image.

I have in front of me a cutting I recently clipped from a national newspaper. It's about an employee of a McDonald's store in Cardiff. He won £1.3 million on the lottery. He hasn't squandered the money. In fact, after buying a new £230,000 home and splashing out on a lavish wedding and holiday in the Canary Islands, he safely invested the rest of the winnings.
    The intriguing thing however, is that he's now back working at the same McDonalds! He earns more every week from his investments than he does from his job!
    Good luck to him. I'm pleased to know he's happy. But this clearly shows that he has not changed or moved from how he saw himself before he had the win. He's obviously comfortable where he still is.

During my years in business I encountered many senior managers and their secretaries, or PA's as they tend to be referred to today. Some of these managers were undoubtedly talented and good at their job. However a fair few were, in my estimation, pretty mediocre and generally incompetent. Nevertheless these under achievers tended to survive in their jobs far longer than perhaps they should have done. In most cases the reason was simple; the secretary knew more about the job than her boss did! She made sure he didn't do anything too stupid and she carefully and subtly orchestrated most of the major decisions.

The irony is that the secretary would be getting paid an annual salary of around £30K and her boss might well have been earning in excess of £150K plus a bonus!!

The problem for the secretaries in these situations was that they only 'saw themselves' as secretaries. Regardless of their superior knowledge and ability they were limited by their perception of themselves.

Because of the way they perceived themselves, they were perceived the same way by others also.

Another example of 'self image' dramatically dictating behaviour is familiar to everyone. We all know at least one person amongst our acquaintances who successfully dieted, lost a considerable amount of weight, and then sadly proceeded to put it all back on again. The problem is they never changed their perception of themselves. They had possibly been overweight for so long that they thought of themselves as being a fat person. Even though wanting to be thinner they continued to see and think of themselves as fat. So gradually their behaviour took them back to being just that.

Not until they change the picture they hold of themselves will they be able to lose the unwanted pounds permanently.

A more positive illustration would be people who made a fortune but then through some unfortunate circumstance lost it, only to recover and make another fortune all over again. One of my close friends did exactly that.

Probably the most famous example of this would be Jeffrey Archer who as a young man lost all his money as a result of a disastrous investment. Subsequently he was forced to resign his position as a Member of Parliament and went on to write his first bestselling novel....Not A Penny More, Not A Penny Less. The rest, as they say, is history! Whether you love him or loathe him you have to admit that he must have a terrific self image as he certainly knows how to bounce back!

Another more recent, and perhaps even better, example of the ability to overcome adversity and make a comeback has been demonstrated by the irrepressible Piers Morgan.

Fired a few years ago from his job as editor of the Daily Mirror he has now hit the 'big time' as a celebrity on both sides of the Atlantic and now hosts top rated TV chat shows in both the US and the UK. There's not much doubt about his self image!

You've heard the expression 'You can't keep a good man

down'.....now you know the reason why.

Recently I met Gerald Ratner.....famous for having jokingly trashed the biggest jewellery business in the UK, of which he was Chief Executive and the major shareholder. He managed to destroy the business through one foolish comment when addressing the Institute of Directors. After several years of feeling sorry for himself and licking his wounds he decided to pick himself up and get back into business.

He tells a brilliant story of how he managed to raise sufficient money (having none left of his own) to build and develop a Health Club in Henley on Thames. He sold it a few years later for a considerable profit and now runs and owns the most successful online jewellery business in the country. He's worth millions again!

All these examples bear testimony to the fact that people always live down to or up to their own self expectations.

I could give you many more illustrations of how our behaviour is always going to be consistent with our self image.

By definition our 'self image' is simply who and what we *imagine* ourselves to be. It doesn't have to become reality. And it's through the power of your imagination that you will gradually succeed in changing your image of yourself.

I mentioned earlier that I had experienced a 'eureka moment' when I suddenly came across this one principle that enabled me to understand why some people succeed where others fail.

At the time of my 'life changing' discovery I was already aware of the importance of developing and maintaining a positive mental attitude and my career was going in the right direction, but it puzzled me that many of my colleagues who had been exposed to the same philosophy were still struggling and hadn't changed.

That's when I read a book and all was revealed!

Here's the story.

In the late forties and fifties, a cosmetic surgeon named Dr. Maxwell Maltz, in the process of doing his work fixing people's scars and facial disfigurements, made a monumental breakthrough discovery for acquiring success, happiness and personal freedom.

During his years of practice, Dr. Maltz observed that plastic surgery produced sudden and dramatic changes in many patients within weeks of an operation. Their growing self esteem and self-confidence mirrored their new physical appearance.

Unfortunately though, in some other cases treating the 'outer scars' failed to cure the 'inner scars', and some patients continued to feel as negatively about themselves as they did before.

This led Dr. Maltz to conclude that many people see themselves inaccurately; their perceptions are distorted by unchallenged and often erroneous beliefs embedded in their sub-conscious mind.

After a decade of counselling hundreds of patients, conducting extensive research on everything from German guided missile technology to hypnosis and testing his own evolving theories, in 1959 Dr. Maltz made one of the most significant discoveries of the 20th century!

The human mind functions much like a goal-seeking device similar to those used to guide missiles on auto-pilot!

The 'automatic goal-seeking device' is the part of the mind that has the power to draw you to whatever you need to accomplish, regardless of whatever obstacles may stand in your way.

You can program it for either success or failure, depending on your self-image. When you learn to develop and improve your self-image you will begin to automatically move towards the achievement of your goals because your sub-conscious mind steers you to them in the same way a guided missile goes to its target!

This was the discovery that changed my life!

There's no rule which states that being born to a poor family means you should stay poor. Nobody is destined to a life of mediocrity just because they were raised by parents whose height of ambition was to be able to afford what they were spending!

My own father once suggested to me as a youngster that becoming a barber wouldn't be a bad idea. He was working on the theory that men would always need to get their hair cut!

I know he had my best interests at heart, but his expectation level for me was clearly restricted by his own beliefs and life experience.

Today there are more young people than ever benefiting from higher education at Universities and Colleges. Sadly though, the majority will never fulfil their true potential because they are 'programmed' for mediocrity.

Most people drift through life on a tide of circumstance, never taking control.

Why? Because they are prisoners of a confining mental picture of themselves.

You *can change* and improve your mental picture. You are never going to 'put yourself down' ever again.

You are going to develop a much more positive self-image. You are going to feel better about yourself than you have ever done before.

For all of us, the mental picture we have of ourselves becomes a self-fulfilling prophecy.

It will dictate all the choices we make.

The only way to change the course of your life is by changing the way you see yourself. This is a choice you have to make!

And the way to change that picture is by changing the way you think and the way you act.

There is no need to be concerned that you are going to have to forfeit your individuality or personality. You will still be you, but a much more successful you!

Look around you. Think of some of the most successful people you know, either personally or because they are famous.

They could range from Bill Gates or Warren Buffet to Chris Hoy, Jessica Ennis or J.K. Rowling. Outstanding business leaders, great sportsmen or women, scientists, singers, actors, writers or designers.

Whatever field they excel in, they all will exhibit very similar qualities and practice the same behaviour patterns that I am going to share with you.

But they haven't relinquished their unique identities!

Be assured, every truly successful person in any field of endeavour has mastered the art of managing themselves.

They manage their emotions and feelings. They manage their time. They control their behaviour. They control their environment. They choose who they associate with. They choose what they read and who and what they listen to. They save and manage their money. They keep score on themselves and constantly strive to do better. They look after their health. They maintain balance in their lives. These are the characteristics of success.

No doubt you already display several of these qualities yourself because you would be unlikely to be reading this otherwise.

But you are going to 'fine tune' these qualities and patterns of behaviour until they become 'second nature'.

You are going to 'programme yourself to succeed'!

Chapter Three

Three Vital Keys to Fulfilling Your Potential

Before discussing the qualities and behaviour patterns that are common to successful people, there are three key areas that we must cover first.

These are critical to achieving and sustaining success. Particularly if achieving your major goals is dependent upon generating income and increasing your assets.

This is equally true whether you have decided to build your own business or have chosen to work your way up in an organisation or professional body.

You will have to address and become skilled in each of these three areas if you are genuinely committed to achieving success and acquiring wealth.

There are no short cuts.

And if you want continued success, and not be a 'flash in the pan', there can be no exceptions.

The three areas that are fundamental to your growth as an individual and the growth of your business are these:-

1. **Managing yourself.**

2. **Managing your business or career.**

3. **Managing your relationships with others.**

1. Managing yourself

Part Two of this book, 'The Complete A-Z Guide to Wealth, Health, Success and Happiness' will have a huge impact on your future. It will affect the way you think and act and behave. It will enable you to move rapidly in the direction you want your life to take.

Because most of Part Two addresses very specifically the keys to

Managing yourself, only one heading, *personality*, is covered here in this section.

Personality

We have already touched upon the fact that each of us has a unique personality. So it's impossible to neatly categorise people. Nevertheless if you have ever taken a simple psychometric test you will know that most of them use four basic personality types.

Even these basic tests demonstrate people's individuality, as there are hundreds of possible outcomes. Nobody is totally one type.

What they are able to do though is to determine basic personality, and my experience is that they are quite accurate.

Here is a version that you can complete in just a few minutes! Even if you've done something like this before, you might like to do it again now.

It's important to try to understand yourself as much as you can. It's also a major step in learning more about understanding others.

But let's be completely clear: **whatever personality type you are has absolutely no bearing on your potential for success!**

The 5 Minute personality test

Instructions:

On each of the ten horizontal lines, put the number 4 by the word that best describes you in that line; a 3 by the word that describes you the next best; a 2 by the next best word; and a 1 by the word that least describes you. You will then have one 4, one 3, one 2, and one 1 on each line. For example, one choice for the first line of words might be:

(3) Likes Having Authority (4) Enthusiastic (2) Sensitive Feelings
(1) Likes Instructions

This is one test you can't fail. Be honest, and you'll discover both your dominant and sub-dominant personality types. None of us are totally one type, but rather a unique combination of all four personality types, with one or two usually taking priority over the others. Each column represents a specific personality type. The column with the highest score is your dominant personality type, while the column with the second highest number will be your sub-dominant type. These two scores reveal the most accurate picture of your natural strengths and weaknesses.

L	O	G	B
Likes Authority	Enthusiastic	Sensitive	Likes Instructions
Takes Charge	Takes Risks	Loyal	Accurate
Determined	Visionary	Calm, Even Keel	Consistent
Enterprising	Likes Talking	Enjoys Routine	Predictable
Competitive	Promoter	Dislikes Change	Practical
Problem Solver	Likes Popularity	Gives in to Others	Factual
Productive	Fun-Loving	Avoids Confrontation	Conscientious
Bold	Likes-Variety	Sympathetic	Perfectionist
Decision Maker	Spontaneous	Nurturing	Detail-Oriented
Persistent	Inspirational	Peacemaker	Analytical
Total "L"	**Total "O"**	**Total "G"**	**Total "B"**

Now plot your total score for each vertical column (L, O, G, B) on the Personality Strengths Survey Chart below. Each letter stands for a particular personality type. The column with the highest score is your dominant personality type. While you are a combination of all four personality types, the two types with the highest scores reveal the most accurate picture of your natural inclinations, strengths, and weaknesses.

Personality Strengths Survey Chart

	L	O	G	B	
40					40
35					35
30					30
25					25
20					20
15					15
10					10
5					5
0					0

Now you've filled in the numbers on the chart let's look at what they mean.

Most tests, similar to this, use these personality type headings: -

Dominance

Influence

Structure

Compliance

However this particular version uses four animals.
L is Lion (Dominance), O is Otter (Influence), G is Golden

Retriever (Structure) and B is Beaver (Compliance)

Don't ask me why. Probably it makes it easier to remember your own profile.

So let's look at the different characteristics.

Lions (Dominance)

Lions are leaders. They are decisive. They love solving problems. They constantly seek adventure and have a low boredom threshold. They are confident and self reliant. They take charge. They are goal oriented, results oriented and achievement driven. They are Risk takers, Self-starters, Persistent and Competitive. They enjoy variety and change. Lions are very independent. They are entrepreneurs.

Some of their weaknesses are that they can be impatient, blunt and direct. They are often poor listeners. They tend to be impulsive and demanding.

Projects may take precedence over people. They are sometimes insensitive.

They are often perceived as being autocratic and dictatorial.

Otters (Influence)

Otters are enthusiasts and excitable. They are fun loving people. They like to influence. Generally they are excellent at networking and usually know lots of people because they are so outgoing. They have a strong need to be liked and receive recognition.

They are good communicators, and are passionate and motivational.

Most people enjoy being around this type of person. They are positive and optimistic. They are people oriented.

Some of their weaknesses are that they can be unrealistic. They dislike detail and hate routine work. They are impulsive and prone to listen to their feelings more than to logic and are quick to react before thinking things through. They can be too talkative. When under pressure they may use their verbal skills to attack.

Golden Retrievers (Structure)

Golden Retrievers are easygoing people. They are very loyal and are excellent team players. They are sensitive to others and know how to show empathy. They put people above projects. They are supportive and reliable. They are wonderful listeners. They make the best friends you could wish for.

They would hate to hurt anyone's feelings. They devote a lot of time helping others and building relationships.

Amongst their weaknesses is the fact that they are indecisive. They dislike confrontation so are often over accommodating. Consequently they may hold grudges rather than bring an issue out into the open.

They may give in under pressure. They need structure and often need time to adjust to change.

Beavers (Compliance)

Beavers are perfectionists. They do things 'by the book'
These are the only people likely to read instruction manuals!
They can be relied upon for accuracy. They tend to be very analytical and methodical. They obey the rules. They have a strong need to do things right.
High standards are important.

Some of their weaknesses include being too hard on themselves. They will never make decisions without all the facts. They like security. They need tasks to be clearly defined.

So you may now have a better understanding of your own personality type. The closer you scored to 40 in your highest column indicates the degree to which you resemble that type.

Remember there is no 'perfect profile' but this knowledge will help you to learn how to play to your strengths and be aware of your weaknesses, which you can modify through learned behaviour.

Another benefit of having completed this exercise is that you can recognise the personality type of other people. It's important to realise that people won't all respond in the same way in identical circumstances.

Accept the fact that not everyone is going to share your point of view or behave as you do.

Clearly you can't go around asking all the people you work or interface with to take a psychometric test to enable you to determine their personality type!

But you can make a conscious effort to observe them so you can start to understand 'where they are coming from'.

We are going to be exploring ways of getting the most out of your relationships with other people a little further on. But let's get back to you for a moment.

When you were reading the characteristics of the Lion, Otter, Golden Retriever and the Beaver, it must have occurred to you that certain personality types suit some occupations better than others.

For example it's unlikely that someone whose dominant personality is that of an Otter would choose to be an accountant or a solicitor. They would probably be more suited to becoming a salesperson or entertainer.

Similarly a Beaver may well be attracted to writing computer software or scientific research.

Golden Retrievers will almost certainly make good teachers.

Now there are no hard and fast rules about this and I could give you plenty of evidence that shows it is dangerous to assume that you should always match jobs to personalities.

Having spent the majority of my career in the Insurance industry I encountered and worked with many actuaries. Typically actuaries tend to display the personality of a Beaver. However I knew several whose personality was more that of a Lion. Not surprisingly a few of them became Chief Executive of their companies!

Being responsible for large numbers of salespeople during my career I can certainly attest to the fact that using personality profiles to try to 'pick winners' proved, as far as I am concerned, to be a total waste of time.

So don't be too influenced by what you have just learned about yourself with regard to your career. The important thing is to acknowledge your strengths and utilise them. Eventually you will find yourself gravitating towards what you are best at. And you'll get other people to do the things you don't enjoy doing.

Which brings us to the second of the three keys.

2. Managing your business or career

Whatever your personal criteria for success might be, it is bound to involve some particular endeavour. In most cases, the quest for success and the material things we associate with wealth and success will revolve around whatever we choose to do for a living.

That's not to say that successes in other areas of our lives are not important. Of course they are. But your job, business, or profession is probably what's going to initially generate the means by which you can afford to live. It will also generate the means for you to put money to work and we'll come to that in great detail later.

Naturally, for the majority of us, relationships with our spouse or partner and our families and our friends are also of paramount importance to living a happy life.

But just at the moment we are going to focus on what you do for a living.

Now here's an important question.

Is what you are currently doing really what you want to be doing?

If the answer is 'Yes' then that's great. You're already on the right track.

But what if the answer is 'No', or even 'I don't know'? Then you may have some serious thinking to do. But don't be discouraged – you are going to get there!

Let's take it step by step. Get some clean sheets of paper and a pen.

All set? Here's what you need to do.

Write down why you decided to do what you're currently doing. Was it just convenient? Did somebody help you to get the job? Did it promise more than has been forthcoming? Is it a stopgap? Did it all start out well and then start to go downhill? Why don't you like it?

Maybe you like it but realise that you will never make a fortune at it. Write down everything that comes into your mind. Be totally honest. Nobody but you is going to see what you have written - so go ahead - be absolutely truthful. Put it all down. What are the plusses? What are the minuses? Are personalities involved? Perhaps you can't stand your boss. Or some of the people you work with.

Now even more honesty is called for. What contributions are *you* making? Have you been an asset or have you just done enough to keep yourself from being fired? Could you have contributed more?

If the answer to that is that you could have contributed more, then why haven't you?

What are your prospects for the future?

This next exercise is really important. Don't read any further until you have done this. It may take half an hour or more. So if you are reading this on a train, or if for any other reason it isn't practical to undertake this exercise right now, bookmark this page and come back to it when you can be on your own with time to focus on this. Please don't read on now. Wait until you have completed this exercise.

There's little point in knowing where you want to be unless you know where you are starting from. And don't worry if you don't know exactly where you want to be either! We are coming to that.

You have now analysed where you currently are. So what's the verdict? Is it possible to achieve what you really want to achieve by staying with what you are doing, or is it time for change?

Remember, in my own circumstances, when I was a hard up salesman it wasn't the fault of the job I was in. There were several people making very good incomes. So it wasn't necessary to change my job. *It was me that had to change.*

However, as I told you earlier, my very first job, after leaving school at sixteen, was as a laboratory assistant. During my first two years there it gradually became apparent to me that I was not enjoying the work and that, even if I continued to study at night school, I was never likely to earn big money.

So I eventually decided the academic life wasn't for me. I don't think it was a terrible loss to the world of scientific research!

At 18 years old I was a bit young to consider starting my own business, but I wanted a career where the rewards were in line with my efforts and results. I didn't want to solely rely on an annual pay increase over which I had little or no control.

Now I'm telling you this for a very good reason.

Hopefully, if you have carried out the exercise of analysing what you are currently doing, you should have arrived at a point where you are soon going to make a decision.

Do you stay or do you leave?

This is what you must take into account.

There are only a few ways by which you are likely to become wealthy. (Assuming that's one of your goals)

1. Generate a relatively high income from what you do for a living and invest a proportion of that income on a regular basis (much more about this later)

2. Marry somebody very rich.

3. Inherit or win a fortune.

4. Rob a bank or engage in some other illegal activity.

For me only the first option was a contender. I did not marry into money. I was not prepared to stake my future on the remote possibility of winning the pools or the lottery (actually there was no lottery in those days.)

My Dad was a lorry driver and my Mum worked at the Co-Op, so they were hardly likely to leave me a fortune. And I didn't want to do anything illegal, especially when considering the consequences of getting caught!

So it had to be a case of generating a high income.

Now many people will tell you that the only way to become fabulously wealthy is to run your own business. Many of my friends and acquaintances have done just that.

In the delightful town in which I live is an incredibly successful entrepreneur who I know well. He founded a company in 1974 that now employs over 1000 people. Twenty-six years after starting his business he sold the company to a huge American organisation for in excess of a Billion Pounds.

His personal shareholding was worth well over £450 million!

What a success story!

Needless to say, not everybody who starts his or her own business is going to make a fortune of those proportions. Most of us wouldn't be prepared to pay the price.

But owning and running your own business isn't necessarily the only way to accumulate a fortune. In fact the entrepreneur I just referred to created multi-millionaires out of several of his key employees through giving them an equity stake in his business when it was still in its growth phase.

These days there are many wealthy people who have generated huge incomes working for successful companies as a result of receiving stock options, bonus plans, or other similar compensation arrangements.

The choice has to be yours. But if you go the company route as an employee make sure the opportunities for advancement are there, and that they are based on merit.

There is nothing to stop you taking one step at a time. It could be that you will work for several companies between now and when you retire. So what? As long as each move is a move in the right direction.

You may also decide that now is not the time to start a business but that you will definitely do so at a later date. Maybe you want to get some experience before you decide to go it alone. There's nothing wrong with that.

But how do you decide where you go from here?

Let me share with you a useful idea that I picked up from reading a book written by Barbara Sher.

The book is called **'I could do anything if I only knew what it was'**

A great title and a super book!

Here's what Barbara Sher suggests you do if you aren't sure what kind of job you would really like and what you would be good at.

(Sorry, but you'll need another sheet or two of paper to do this.)

Instead of listing all the things you might want in a job, or what kind of business you think would appeal to you, you are going to do exactly the opposite!

Amazingly it's often difficult to be specific about what we truly want, but we have less difficulty in identifying what we don't want.

So, if you've got your sheet of paper ready, you can start by writing the heading: **'Everything I would really hate in a job'.**

Now describe in great detail what you would consider to be a total nightmare job.
    For example it could go something like this: -

"I would hate to work in a noisy factory that has no natural light and which is also dirty and smells horrible; where the work is mind-numbingly boring.
    The pay is poor and I have to work loads of overtime to try to earn enough to pay the bills.
    There's no travel involved. Promotion prospects are based on length of service and nothing to do with ability.
    Nobody ever consults me for my opinion. We never have the opportunity to make any suggestions as to how the business could be improved.
    Communication from management as to how we are doing is non-existent and nobody ever receives any recognition...."

By now you get the idea.
    Put down as much as you can. Let your imagination run free!

Once you have concluded this list, with all the features you can possibly think of that would really be anathema to you, take another sheet of paper.

This time you can head it **'My idea of the perfect job'**

All you have to do is to take the job description you just wrote and express the exact opposite.
    By doing it this way you will find that you have crystallised very specifically the outline of your perfect job, career or business.
    Do please try this. You'll be surprised at how effective it is.

Hopefully by now you are beginning to focus on the future and are moving towards making some important career decisions.
    However it's important that you read this entire book before you actually start to take action.
    We want to make sure you are fully equipped to take full advantage of the opportunities you are going to be able to choose from.

But before we move on to the third of the 'three keys to success', I want to stress a most important issue with regard to 'managing your business'. It's this: -

You have to know what you are doing!

Let me elaborate by using a true example.

I was talking a few years ago to two men who own a business providing and installing top of the range bathrooms. They had just done an excellent job of installing a new shower in our home which had involved taking out an old one, changing the plumbing, replacing the wall tiles and fitting a new shower door. My wife and I were delighted with the outcome. These guys had definitely exceeded our expectations.

Now this pair had only recently moved to the town where we live and had taken over an existing bathroom business.

So, being inquisitive, I asked them what had happened to the previous owner.

'He went bankrupt' they told me! (They possibly meant that he simply ran out of money).

This seemed quite surprising; since we live in one of the most affluent areas in England, where there are plenty of very expensive houses and stacks of people who can easily afford to spend money on improving their homes.

So I probed a bit further.

"Well he knew nothing about the business. He had never been out on a job in his life. He had no idea how to quote accurately or how to organise a project, and he had no background in bathroom design".

In other words he hadn't developed any real 'know how' about the business he was in! He was totally out of his depth and was pouring good money after bad. He eventually ran out of cash and went out of business, having sustained a huge loss. (The two guys who had taken over the business actually told me how much, but I don't think it's appropriate for me to divulge the amount. But believe me, it was substantial!).

So what's the moral here? Pretty obvious of course.

Don't start or buy a business you know nothing about!

It's a well-known fact that opening a restaurant is one of the most hazardous business risks you could take. There are more failed restaurants than any other single type of business failure. The reason is plain. People think that because they eat out regularly and they can cook, they are equipped to succeed as restaurateurs. No way!

There are dozens of issues you must be aware of in running any catering venture and the only way to acquire enough essential knowledge is to work in several successful restaurants long enough to have really 'learned the ropes'.

The two partners, Paul and Steve, who own the Bathroom business will definitely succeed. They know the business from beginning to end. They have spent years developing the 'know how'. They are experts.

So if you decide to go into business on your own account for goodness sake get as much relevant experience as you possibly can before you start up for yourself.

If on the other hand you prefer to work for an employer the same principles apply.

Do everything you can to become an expert in your field. Be prepared to learn, observe, ask questions, and study.

Keep in mind that most of your contemporaries won't be prepared to pay the price to do those things.

So it will be easy to compete with them!

Show that you are an 'extra-miler'. It won't be long before you get noticed.

I'm confident that if you follow the steps being outlined, as you continue reading this, your rise through your company can be meteoric. If that doesn't happen you should move to another company. Find an employer who knows how to value outstanding employees.

Because outstanding is what you are going to become!

3. Managing your relationships with others

Walk into any large bookstore, Waterstones for example, and go into the non-fiction area. Stroll around for ten minutes or so and look at the thousands of books covering an endless variety of subjects. No doubt you will find it to be as intimidating an experience as I do.

The fact is, when we consider the huge quantity of knowledge and wisdom that has accumulated over the centuries, it's impossible for any one person to master anything but just a tiny fraction of this overwhelming amount of information.

So it's easy to realise that you will never know everything, and that you can only ever become an expert in a few things at most.

You don't have to be a genius to achieve your dreams and you don't have to be good at all the things that are critical to your specific goals.

That's why you will need to enlist the help of other people.

The skills and expertise of others are going to be an essential ingredient of your success.

They are going to be the resources that you will call upon as your business or career develops.

Dependent on the type of venture you engage in, you are also likely to need other people's efforts and labour as well as their knowledge.

One thing, of which you can be sure, is that you'll never get to where you want to be under entirely your own steam.

So, since you are going to be harnessing the power of other people, it's vital you get the best from them.

The relationships you develop will be on several levels.

Some people will be virtual partners. Not in the financial sense necessarily, where they share and work in your business, but in the sense that they provide advice and services.

For example if you are building your own business, you are going to need banking facilities and an accountant. Possibly you will need legal advice. You may decide to outsource some administrative functions.

You will probably require providers and suppliers of products and services.

These people won't be on your payroll, but they can have a huge impact on your success or failure.

So look upon them as partners.

Select them carefully. Treat them with respect. Don't ever be indifferent to them.

The chances are that if you are running your own business, you will also employ people. If you are working for someone else you will have colleagues. You'll also have a boss. You may well have people reporting directly to you.

And in all probability you will have clients or customers!

Consequently, how good you are at understanding and responding to the needs, motivations and behaviour of the people you work with, regardless of on what basis, is going to be a significant factor in achieving your goals.

Earlier, when we were talking about personality, we covered the different characteristics of the four personality types.

The statement which follows should not be considered as contradictory to the fact that people have significantly different personalities.

In spite of differing personalities, and regardless of age, sex, colour and creed, the similarities between people are far greater than the differences!

During my years as an Insurance Company executive, in addition to spending much of my time in the UK, I also briefly lived and worked in America. Furthermore, I spent time working with Canadians, as well as making a few business trips to Australia.

More recently I have worked in many countries in South East Asia and much of Central Europe and Russia.

Although there are significant differences in each of these countries, I have learned that, regardless of nationality and origin, **most people intrinsically have the same fundamental reasons for doing or not doing things.**

Naturally it's essential to acknowledge that there are obvious cultural differences, and that each country has its own customs and protocols, but it didn't take me long to establish that people in Asia experience much the same emotions and have similar motivations and aspirations as we in the West do.

So before we move on to the next section, which is the heart of what will put you on the road to success, it may be worthwhile covering some basic but relevant facts you should know about people.

Normally I'm not big on theory, and books that are filled with diagrams and charts generally leave me cold. They tend to be written by academics that have never had to put any of their theories into actual practice!

Having said that however, there is a well-known and respected theory about people that I've found to be exceedingly accurate and which has stood the test of time; perhaps you are familiar with it.

It's called 'Maslow's hierarchy of needs'

Here's what Maslow teaches us.

There are five levels in the hierarchy and it's impossible to move up to the next level until the previous ones have been satisfied.

The first level is: - **Basic survival.**

Man's most basic need is to survive! So, if faced with danger or threat, he will think of nothing else other than how to deal with whatever poses that danger. His absolute attention will be given to removing or overcoming whatever is endangering him or his family. He also needs to be sure of finding food in order not to starve. He will fight hard to survive!

The second level is: - **Safety and security.**

Having dealt with the danger he will then turn his attention to finding shelter and safety.

Somewhere secure to live, with food and warmth and a bed to sleep in.

The third level is: - **Belonging**

Provided that he now feels safe and secure and is able to provide food and the basic essentials, he now feels the need to belong. He wants companionship and to belong to a group. He also wants to be loved.

This is why, in primitive societies, tribes were formed, and why today we still get passionate about our football teams etc.

People need and love to be part of something.

This was wonderfully evident in the UK when we hosted the Olympic Games.

London 2012 generated huge national pride and fervour. A genuine feeling of togetherness.

This inherent driving force is a double-edged sword. It is how communities that work together for the benefit of its members are created; but it has also been the cause of countless wars over religion and territory throughout the ages.

The fourth level is: - **Ego**

This is now where being just a member of a group isn't enough. Now he wants recognition and esteem. Possibly even power.

Lots of people never get to this level, they just dream about it!

It's a popular misconception that money is a great motivator. But in reality, it's not so much the money, it's more about what money can buy!

Large and impressive houses, prestigious cars, fashionable clothes; these are some of the things that many achievers aspire to, because it is a way of 'keeping score'.

This how we compete and prove to others how well we are doing.

Never underestimate the need for recognition. Some people display this need more than others. They are the egoists and extroverts who have an insatiable appetite for attention, praise and adulation.

But don't be fooled by the 'shrinking violets'. They too need the esteem of others.

We often are told that greed is a powerful motivator. That's primarily because greed is a manifestation of a desire for money to buy and exhibit the trappings of the rich and successful.....which brings us back to recognition.

Recognition is one of the most potent motivators there is.

The fifth and final level is: - **Self Actualisation** (Maslow's expression - not mine!)

This is the level you should ultimately be striving for. ***Freedom!***

The freedom to do practically whatever you want, whenever you want, and however you want; provided of course that it's legal and doesn't violate the rights of other people.

You are no longer forced to do what somebody else tells you to do.

If you continue to work it's because you want to rather than have to.

Now you have reached the point where you can express yourself however you wish. You are no longer too concerned about how others see you. You have risen above that.

This is the pinnacle of achievement!

Since the majority of people you are likely to encounter have moved on from levels one and two, it should be a fundamental of understanding yourself and others that the needs of levels three and four are going to be paramount.

Being part of a team and the need for the esteem and respect of others are very powerful drivers.

We are getting close to the point where we are going to delve into the qualities and characteristics of highly successful people. But before we do there are a few more bits of advice about people that I'd like to hand on.

Firstly don't get frustrated if some people fail to live up to your expectations. Most of them will not be as committed as you are, and not prepared to work as hard. Be grateful!

If they were just like you it would be so much harder for you to be successful. Too many people would be competing with you!

The fact that you have come this far is clear evidence that you have what it takes to rise above the pack.

However, if you embrace the principles and strategies practised by high achievers, you will have no problem in getting superior performances from mediocre people.

The next critical issue is this. **You must surround yourself with quality people.**

I'm not talking about an army. But I am talking about those who will be closest to you.

Whether you are going to be building a business for yourself or running a department in a company, it is essential that you recruit winners.

All the most successful business leaders I know readily testify as to how much they owe their success to the people they assembled around them.

Never be afraid to bring people in who you suspect may be better than yourself. They will only push you further in the direction you want to go.

Alternatively, if you surround yourself with sycophants who make you feel good because they constantly pander to your ego, you'd better brace yourself. Failure will be just around the corner.

As I've mentioned several times now, nobody succeeds without a great deal of help from others. So choose wisely.

Finally, before we move to the next section, there is one more important request for when you hit the big-time in business.

Share the wealth!

If, as your business grows and prospers, you try to keep the wealth all to yourself, you will quickly disenchant the very people who have been instrumental in helping you get where you are.

They will only be too aware of their own worth, and if they aren't rewarded accordingly they will be off. Headhunters are constantly on the prowl and will jump at the chance of capturing your best people.

Anyway what's wrong with making other people rich?

You may be concerned that your key employees may lose focus if they become independently wealthy and were no longer hungry. That won't happen. You'll find they will be more loyal than ever and motivated to work even harder, as they will no longer be distracted or anxious regarding their financial situation.

"You can get everything you want out of life if you help enough people get what they want out of life" (Zig Ziglar)

So far we have talked a lot about the importance of your 'self-image'. By the way, please don't confuse 'self image' with self esteem. Self esteem is how you *feel* about yourself and can readily and frequently change according to prevailing circumstances. For example, if somebody compliments you on how you look, or on something you have accomplished, your self esteem will almost certainly rise. On the other hand criticism may well lower your self esteem.

Self esteem and 'self-image' are indeed linked in as much that if you have a very positive 'self image' it is certain that your self esteem will be high most of the time, and it would be unlikely that anyone could easily damage it. It follows therefore that a poor 'self-image' will result in low self esteem.

So self-esteem is how you *feel* about yourself and 'self-image' is how you *see* yourself.

Since you have had a mental picture of yourself from the time you were growing up, this is going be quite hard for you to change, but the good news is that you can and you will!

Part two of this book is written in a way that will enable you to refer back to it frequently and easily. I have endeavoured to cover the entire A – Z of the practices, behaviours and attitudes which characterise success. There are many Universal Principles contained in this section and you must try to relate them to yourself. These principles are timeless and apply equally regardless of culture, religion, sex or creed. Many people, who are truly successful in life, practice some of these principles without even knowing.

It really doesn't matter whether you practice them consciously or without realising, they will work for you just the same.

You'll also notice some repetition. No doubt you've observed that already! I make no apologies however, as repetition is crucial to learning.

Through the acceptance and constant practice of these principles you will dramatically improve the mental picture you hold of yourself. You will like yourself more than you do today. You will start to attract the things you want to achieve and acquire. You will have more confidence, more energy and more zest for life. You will move closer to fulfilling your true potential.

Every day will be an exciting adventure!

Part Two

The A-Z Guide to Wealth, Health, Success and Happiness

All you will ever need to know to become a high flyer

The principles and philosophy practised and characterised by the most successful people in all walks of life are documented in simple alphabetical order. So they don't follow a particular sequence of priorities. You will easily detect those that are most vital to your success. All are important…but some are more important than others!

Several of the most vital ingredients for success will be repeated throughout these pages. That's by design. Repetition, as you already know, is a major key to learning!

A

ACTION

Without it nothing happens.

That's a statement of the obvious. **Yet failure to act is the reason most people never realise their dreams!** The vital key to achieving anything and everything is to at least get started!

In this world it isn't so much what you know that counts. It's what you do!

The world is full of educated derelicts.

Why do so many people continually put things off? Fear of failure would rank high. It's safer not to set out to accomplish something, that way there's no danger of embarrassment if we don't succeed.

Lack of action may also stem from the fact that most people don't like change.

Another reason for putting things off is that the task or goal may seem so formidable we don't know where to start – so we don't!

Additionally it's important to recognise that **instant gratification is more enticing than remote reward.**

The time required for achieving some objectives is often so far away that it seems starting today or tomorrow isn't going to make much difference, so tomorrow will do!

Saving money is a classic example. If you are already overdrawn at the bank, have debit balances on your credit cards and bank loan commitments, it would seem a bit futile to start saving to become independently wealthy.

But were you to do so, even if you started with only a modest amount such as five pounds a day, you would be taking a gigantic step towards acquiring wealth. And, what is so crucially important, is that you would be developing a valuable habit that will eventually transform your life.

If this applies to you, and you are not saving regularly, then let me urge you to ignore the advice that many people may give which is to get out of debt before starting to save. What you need to develop is the savings habit. And you need to start now!

It doesn't matter one bit that the interest you earn on your savings will be much less than you are paying on your debts. *If you don't start saving now I predict that you will probably never get out of debt!*

Thousands upon thousands of people who will retire this year have less than £2000 in savings and only their paltry state pensions to keep them. **If only they had *acted* when they thought about saving.** You'll be amazed at what the miracle of time and compound interest can do.

You'll find a 'mind-blowing' example, as you read on, of the incredible outcome of regular saving and investment.

Quite a thought for smokers who effectively burn all that money instead of tucking it away!

How many overweight people needing to lose a stone or two are expert at putting off the start of a diet?

"After the weekend." "After my holiday." "I'll begin straight after Christmas." "Hang on, I forgot the New Year's Eve Party, I'll begin on January 1st, Oh no, we've got the office Dinner Dance the following Saturday, I'll begin immediately after that"…and so on and so on!

If you would break down that big goal into smaller and easier to achieve goals, your motivation will increase considerably.

Losing just a pound a week for 28 weeks is a lot easier to contemplate, and commit to, than losing 2 stones!

"A journey of 1,000 miles begins with a single step", says the famous proverb.

Successful people are ACTION people; they have developed a DO IT NOW approach.

W.Clement Stone who co-authored with Napoleon Hill 'Success through a Positive Mental Attitude' attributes the huge success he enjoyed and the massive fortune he made to just those three words **'Do it now!'**

And he lived to be a hundred years old by the way!

Think of something simple that you've been intending to do ... but as yet have still to get around to.

A letter to be written to a friend or relative ... a repair job in the house... tidying up the garage ... sorting out the drawer full of clothes you never wear.

AND DO IT TODAY!

In fact don't read on until you have acted!

Put this book down and go and do something that you've been putting off.

Go on. Do it now!

Welcome back.

Now, providing you've not cheated, you probably feel quite good.

But what else have you been procrastinating over?

Write a 'Things To Do List'. Set a reasonable time limit. No longer than two weeks. And do everything on the list.

Once you have got the momentum going you will find it easy to take the next step which is to write a 'things to do list' every day.

There will be times that you won't get everything done on the day so just simply write any outstanding tasks on the next day's list.

Another benefit of this habit becoming a way of life is that you'll never forget anything you are supposed to do or have promised to do.

There is some authenticated research done (Harvard University) that incontrovertibly links this as being one of the most common habits of the top three per cent of achievers whose careers have been followed since graduating from Harvard.

If you will really apply yourself to this simple exercise you'll take very significant steps towards permanently changing your life.

You will learn to break the habit most typical of failures; Procrastination.

One of the most powerful sayings I learned years ago is that, *'successful people are people who have developed the habit of doing the things that failures don't like doing'*

PURPOSEFUL ACTIVITY is one of the major keys to success.

ACT...GET STARTED...OVERCOME INERTIA...DO IT NOW!

ABILITY

Don't believe anybody who tells you "You can be anything you want to be, and do anything you want to do." It simply isn't true.
Unless it's believable it won't be achievable.

Much as I might wish to, I'm never going to win the men's singles at Wimbledon or sing on stage at the Royal Opera House or play football for England.
There are probably a lot of things you don't have the ability to do either. And never will.

But think how many things you could do if you were prepared to acquire the necessary skills and knowledge.

Think what you could achieve if only you were prepared to practice and then practice some more.
Look at the work put in by top sportsmen and sportswomen in order to become outstanding performers.
Most things are within your grasp if you are prepared to pay the price to learn and to practice hard.

Nobody was born a surgeon, or an airline pilot, or a master craftsman, or a brilliant salesperson, or a great golfer, or a great anything come to that.
It takes effort and dedication.

You are going to be amazed at what you can do, simply by making up your mind to develop your ability to do it!

AMBITION

You will find it a whole lot easier to get into action and to stay motivated if you develop a burning desire to achieve something.

People with no ambition are simply drifting along. Taking whatever life doles out to them; which won't be much.
So decide now, what is the most important thing you want to do with your life in the next few years?

Don't go any further without deciding upon at least one major accomplishment that you're determined to strive for. (You should already have done this as suggested right at the beginning of this book.)
If you didn't do it then you *must* do it now. If you read on without doing this you'll be seriously selling yourself short. You'll be acting just like most failures…all good intentions but no action.

It doesn't have to be your life's work you are deciding on here. If you're still relatively young that may be difficult to do at this stage. But you must have something that is going to drive you forward. A mission that excites and enthuses you.
Whatever that may be, write it down now.

We will go into detail as to just how vitally important this process is as we continue this journey.

ATTITUDE

Before putting any of this in writing I attempted to come up with an order of priority as to what were the most important issues in achieving success. I found it difficult to decide.

This led me to take the approach of covering all the qualities, behaviours and characteristics, which will guarantee you success, simply in A to Z order.
However it's quite a coincidence that *five of the seven most important ingredients for success all begin with A!*

(In case you're wondering, they are Attitude, Ambition, Action, Ability and Accountability)

You'll know what the other two are in due course.
That's not to say that you can skip reading from B to Z!

We have already established that one of the major keys to success is purposeful **activity.** Here is the most important one of all ...

POSITIVE ATTITUDE!

Positive People Get Positive Results

But what is a positive attitude? – And how do you acquire and maintain it?

It's important to know how to develop it within yourself before trying to develop it in others.

Simply stated, a positive attitude is a composite of positive characteristics.

Here are a few examples: -

- Honesty as opposed to dishonesty.

- Generosity as opposed to meanness.

- Kindness as opposed to spitefulness.

- Humour as opposed to being humourless.

- Friendliness as opposed to aggression.

- Optimism as opposed to pessimism.

- Energetic as opposed to lethargic.

- A 'can do, will try' approach as opposed to 'can't do, won't bother to try' attitude.

- A happy disposition as opposed to a miserable one.

- Tactful as opposed to tactless.

- Enthusiasm as opposed to indifference.

- Consideration as opposed to being inconsiderate.

- Courage as opposed to cowardice.

- Willingness as opposed to unwillingness.

- Good tempered as opposed to bad tempered.

Nobody's perfect, so each of us may need to work hard at developing and improving several of these characteristics.

Because 'positive people' display most of these qualities most of the time, they are a pleasure to be around. They give off 'good vibes'. They are doers. They have learned to keep their minds focused on what they want and off the things they don't want. They have charisma. They are magnetic.

These are people who 'see a glass as being half full instead of half empty'

Now you won't change your entire thinking overnight. So don't expect to.

You can't be a 'phoney' about this. Telling yourself that you can do something, when deep down you don't believe you can, is not going to work. That's why you need to work on building your confidence and improving your self-image.

However, you must start to form the habit of blocking out negative thoughts…. especially about yourself.

As you practice many of the principles in this book your confidence will grow, together with your self-esteem.

As a result you will automatically appear to be more positive. **Because you *will* be more positive.**

There is an amazing fact about positive thinking which I know to be true:

I remember my father telling me, after he had retired, that he had bought a new television set. I asked him if he bought a colour one since colour TV was still in its infancy at the time. (This was many years ago now.)

"No I got another black and white one because I read in the newspaper that one in twenty colour TV's blow up" he replied.

"Then why didn't you buy one of the nineteen that isn't going to blow up?" I asked.

It was a flippant question perhaps, but relevant nevertheless.

My dad would have almost certainly however bought the wrong one had he bought a colour TV ...*because he would have expected to*!

Positive thinkers have a positive expectancy, they 'think lucky' and consequently they get lucky. People with positive attitudes have learned to turn adversity into opportunity.

My father was a lovely man but sadly he often expected the worst, which almost certainly prevented him from doing many of the things he might otherwise have done.

On another occasion I clearly recall telling my Dad that I had booked to go on holiday later that year.

"Well don't look forward to it too much" was his well-meaning advice.

"Why ever not" I wanted to know.

"Because if anything happens, and you can't go, you won't be too disappointed" was his reply!

Sadly that kind of logic was not just the preserve of many working class people who were living in difficult times following the Second World War, many people still think that way today without realising how destructive a negative attitude can be. They constantly look for the downside. They don't understand that they are almost willing their fears to become a self-fulfilling prophecy.

Please believe me, there really is a 'magic' that actually attracts the good things to positive people. Conversely negative people seem able to attract all the problems and difficulties life has to offer.

Don't ask me how this works because frankly I can't tell you. **But it is a universal force that truly exists...of that I can assure you.**

Positive people enjoy better health than negative people.

Positive thinkers look for the good in situations and in people, and they generally find it.

They get the best out of life because they put the most into it.

I could share story after story with you drawn both from personal experience and that of others. However, I didn't set out to write a whole manual on positive thinking. I just have to stress that it is an absolute requirement to becoming successful. You must always strive to maintain a positive attitude and do everything you can to help others acquire the same.

ACCOUNTABILITY

Having to account for our actions (or lack of them) forces most of us to do our job as well as we know how.
    Without accountability there is no real motivation.
    Keeping score on how you are doing is critically important.

Senior management have to account to the company's shareholders, middle management have to account to senior management, etc. Everybody requires structure and deserves to know exactly what is required of them.

Everybody also needs, and responds to, recognition for a job well done. Imagine going out to a golf course to practice on your own, and for the first (and perhaps only) time in your life you hit a hole in one. And nobody was there to see you do it! Wouldn't that be just a golfer's worst nightmare!

If your current circumstances mean that you only account to yourself, then you should find a mentor you can share your plans with. Be sure to choose somebody who you would rather impress than disappoint.
    This is really important.

Never underestimate the need we all have for recognition and accountability.

ADVERSITY

There's not a single person who ever walked on this planet who hasn't encountered times of crisis.
    Wealth may make life a lot more pleasant and enjoyable, but it doesn't protect you from the realities of life. Nor will position or power.

We all experience tough times.

There is always something unexpected that can throw you off course. Accidents, bereavement, breakdown of relationships, being a victim of crime, making a bad business decision, changes in legislation, natural disasters.

In both your personal life and your business life you are going to be faced with some occurrences that you would much rather have done without!

Now this isn't being negative and isn't contradictory to what you just read under the heading of Attitude.

Positive people don't live with their heads in the sand. They acknowledge that from time to time they will have to deal with a difficult situation that they either didn't or couldn't foresee.

But what makes the difference is the way they react to the crisis!

Negative people feel sorry for themselves. They may look for others to blame. They may simply give up trying to resolve the situation.

But winners react differently!

They assess the situation with a solution-based approach. They quickly decide if anything can be done. If there is, they get into action. However if there is nothing that can be done to change the situation they pick themselves up and move on.

Because they have learned this one very significant principle.

Every adversity carries with it the seed of an equivalent or greater benefit, if you look for it with a positive mental attitude.

This was taught to me when I was in my mid twenties and, from many of my own experiences, I can testify to the truth of this powerful maxim.

My mother expressed the same principle somewhat differently by saying "Every cloud has a silver lining"

In all probability you can think back to situations in your own life where the evidence of this can be recognised. Perhaps you were made redundant and went on to get a better job for example.

"It seemed like a disaster at the time but looking back it was a blessing in disguise."

How many times have you heard somebody say something like this? Maybe you've had cause to say something similar yourself.

So whenever faced with a problem or challenge, however catastrophic it may seem at the time, get into the habit of looking for what good may ultimately emerge. And expect it to do so.

Take on board this little quote I once heard. "Some people would consider a broken arm to be an accident but others would regard it as an adventure!"

ADVICE

There will be many occasions where you should seek advice, but first make absolutely certain that the source is qualified to give it!

Think very carefully before giving advice yourself ... there's just an outside chance that someone may take it!

Don't give it unless you really know what you are talking about, and you've been asked to, and keep in mind that a lot of people would be much more successful if they simply heeded the advice they regularly give others.

APOLOGIES

There's one thing of which we can be sure. We are sometimes wrong! Like it or not. And there's only one thing to do ... apologise. Regardless of whether it's over a minor point or a major issue, something of no consequence, or a disastrous decision. Apologise!

Then, according to the circumstances, there may be urgent action, (that word *action* again), required to put things right... or as right as possible.

To apologise is not demeaning ... it's character building. Don't grovel or be self-depreciating ... just simply admit your mistake, say sorry and make amends as necessary.

Do it freely, simply and without trying to justify or rationalise. You won't lose respect ... you'll earn it!

APPEARANCE

You never get a second chance to make a first impression! An old

cliché I'll admit. But don't underestimate its importance.
Make sure that you portray the right image.

All of us tend to make quick judgements about people when meeting them for the first time. Perhaps we shouldn't be so ready to jump to conclusions. But we nearly always do.
So pay attention to detail. It can be the little things that can make a difference.
Clean fingernails that haven't been bitten for example.

Ask any woman and she'll tell you that many men let themselves down because their shoes need cleaning!
It amazes me how many people travel to work in trains or in their cars, and even on planes, wearing their jackets. By the time they get to wherever they are going the backs of their jackets are full of creases! You'll look so much better if you take off your jacket when travelling and put it on the back seat or an overhead rack.

Even in the current climate of 'dressing down' and 'business casual' it's still important to look clean and fresh. Knowing you look good will always have a terrific impact on your self-esteem.
It's important to dress for success.
But remember, of all the things you wear, your expression is the most important.

ARGUMENTS

I have to admit here to one of my weaknesses. I still have to guard against it. If you recognise yourself as sharing this trait – pay attention!
It's simply that regardless of how unimportant or trivial the point may have been, if I was convinced that I was right I hated to give up or give in. I used to feel compelled to prove that I'm right.
Because I can be forceful, persuasive and persistent I used to 'win' lots of arguments. The trouble is I suspect that I lost quite a few friends in the process!

Wasn't it Abraham Lincoln who said something like, "What does it matter if one concedes seven points in order to win the eighth, if the eighth is the most important?

The fact is you don't win anything if you alienate other people.

Most arguments need never occur.

ATTENTION

Pay it! Especially in one-on-one situations.

If you have a limited attention span, tackle the tough jobs first.
 Also try breaking your various activities down into time spans you can live with. Once you cease to pay attention to what you are doing ... or what someone is saying ... you cease to be effective.
 Attention to detail is also essential. How would you feel about flying with an airline that didn't pay close attention to detail?
 So often that little extra effort makes all the difference.

AVERAGE

Don't ever take comfort in being average! You may be the best of the worst ... but you will also be the worst of the best!

AVAILABILITY

Many years ago I was holding a staff meeting with the five key District Managers in my sales Region. At the time we were running hot and getting some terrific results – we had enjoyed being the number one Region in the UK for several years.
 We held these staff meetings about once a month for the purpose of planning, exchanging ideas, and monitoring our results.
 They were a great group and always fun to be with. I always looked forward to these meetings. Especially when things were going great.
 At the end of this particular day one of the managers, Roy, asked me if I'd drop him off at the local garage to collect his car which had been serviced.
 On the way there I was enthusing about our results and saying what a great meeting we'd had. He looked at me and in a surprisingly reproachful manner said, "It may have been a great meeting from your point of view but it wasn't from mine"
 Taken aback I asked him what he meant.
 "Well", he replied, "you only ever seem to think of us as a team these days. When was the last time you sat down and talked to me on my own?"

From that episode you can be sure I learned a very valuable and vital lesson. As much as team building is important, and as much as most of us love to be part of a winning team, we all want to be treated as individuals too.

I stupidly had stopped making myself available to the people on my team on a one to one basis.

I will always be grateful to Roy for the lesson I learned that day.

Since then I made sure that I took time to get together regularly with each of my key people individually, as well as in a group.

If you are a parent the same thing applies. Your children need to have your undivided attention all to themselves from time to time. Don't think that by spending a lot of time with your family as a unit that that's sufficient.

I'm pleased to say that Roy continued, until he recently retired, to be an outstanding Sales Executive who made many significant contributions to the company we worked for and to the many people who worked with him.

AUTOBIOGRAPHIES

You'll find they aren't written by failures!

Reading autobiographies of famous and successful people is a brilliant and entertaining way of learning many of the principles you need to recognise if you want to get the best out of yourself.

It's also very reassuring to know that, almost without exception, the authors came from normal and often working class backgrounds.

Amongst those I have read is Nelson Mandela's 'Long Walk to Freedom' which is an inspiration. Backgrounds don't come much tougher than having been a black man in South Africa during the majority of the twentieth century.

Yet he ultimately became a universally acclaimed leader on the World stage.

Over the years I've read dozens of autobiographies and I've enjoyed and learned from them all.

B

BALANCE

Much of the emphasis of what we've talked about so far has been on making money and acquiring wealth. In all probability it's the main reason you bought this book. And that's fine. You already know that I attach a great deal of importance to money and I'd find it difficult to go back to the days when I was struggling.

However life is about much more than just money; it's important to maintain a proper balance. Failure to do so may well have consequences that will adversely affect your happiness.

Make sure you attach equal importance to your relationships with your spouse or partner and your children. Make time to enjoy being with friends. Take care of your emotional and spiritual needs. Look after your health and keep yourself fit. Continue your personal development. Work on your business or career. Take holidays and leisure time to relax and have fun.
This is what life is about.

BELIEF

If you don't believe in yourself it's hardly likely that anyone else will.

If you don't believe in what you are doing – you won't do it well. Most important – if anyone ever finds you lied to them they will never be able to completely believe in you again. Don't ever risk jeopardising your believability.

The stark reality about belief is that whatever you do or don't believe is going to impact almost everything you do.

It will dictate your actions. It will affect your emotions. It will control your destiny.

Now I appreciate that right now it may be difficult for you to believe that are going to become independently wealthy. Especially if you are up to your neck in debt.

But that's primarily because you don't know precisely how you are going to get there.

So what! Does that mean that you can't?
Of course it doesn't!
Take it one step at a time.

Naturally you may have a hard time getting your head round being worth two or three million pounds. But you should have no problem believing you can substantially increase your current income by thirty, forty or fifty percent or more in the next couple of years, regardless of how much or how little you are presently making.

If you don't believe that's possible then you'd better go back to the beginning of this book and start all over. You clearly haven't been paying attention.

You have as much right as anybody to a happy and fulfilling life. You are as worthy as the next person.

As you progress forward, setting and achieving perhaps only modest goals to begin with, you will find it so much easier to raise your belief level as to what you are truly capable of becoming.

BEHAVIOUR

It's been my observation that it's difficult to change basic personality. Personality seems to be set almost from birth and becomes well developed by the time we reach six or seven years old.

What can be changed or modified though, is the way we behave. By doing so, small and gradual changes in our personality may begin to occur.

Although much of what we do, or the way we react in certain situations is now instinctive, it can be changed through making a conscious effort.

We have total control over the way we behave. And consequently must take total responsibility for our behaviour.

Losing one's temper easily… sulking or being 'moody'… consistently being late… being suspicious and sceptical… being argumentative… being disorganised… procrastinating etc. These are all behaviour patterns that have been learned, and which may have become habits; often since childhood.

But you are not a prisoner of those traits. Simply a victim.

You have the power to change those attitudes and habits.

It's not acceptable to say, "I can't help it. That's just the way I am."
Or, "It's not my fault I take after my father (or mother)."
Frankly that's simply a cop-out.

You may have learned that kind of behaviour from somebody when you were growing up, but that doesn't mean you have to emulate it for the rest of your life!

So examine your behaviour patterns and determine what you do that may be to your detriment, and resolve to start making a conscious effort to change. It will take some time and won't always be easy. But it will certainly be worth the effort!

BRAINS

Brains are very much like the bodies in which they reside… they need nourishment and regular exercise. In just the same way you should eat a healthy diet you should endeavour to feed your mind with positive thoughts and suggestion.

What you put in is what you'll get out.
   Make sure you associate with positive people. Pay no attention to moaners and whiners. Read other self-development books. Listen to self-development CDs. You may want to get in the habit of giving your brain a daily workout by doing a Crossword or a Sudoku puzzle or a Codeword puzzle.

BULLIES

Bullies are cowards. Simple as that. If you are ever a victim stand up for yourself and don't allow it. Almost invariably the bully will back down.
   Never ever be guilty yourself of trying tactics of intimidation to get results. It may work briefly but you will definitely get your comeuppance. And serve you right too!

BUSINESS

For most of us that's what we are in. It's all about people ... products ... processes ... production ... profits ... cash flow ... budgets ... performance ... marketing and market share ... revenue ... growth ... etc.

Each business has its own individual set of rules to be learned and to be adhered to. But all businesses share a great deal in common – they require the acquisition, management and development of good people. Also remember that business improves when people improve. So do everything you can to train, coach, develop, stretch and inspire your employees.

For most businesses the cost of salaries is by far the largest overhead and the people they employ are the company's biggest asset. Doesn't it make sense then to do everything possible in terms of training, development and motivation to get the very best out of every employee?

Too many businesses tend to focus on processes instead of people. In many cases productivity, and subsequently profit, could be substantially improved if more attention were paid to creating an environment in which people were taught and encouraged to perform at their very best.

C

CHANGE

Many people experience a certain amount of stress and anxiety when confronted with change.

Yet change can often be a source of renewed enthusiasm and excitement.

Many of us look forward to doing new things, learning new skills, seeing new places, meeting new people, and so on.

If you manage people in your job, and need to make changes in the way those people work, try to give some lead in time where possible. Offer them the opportunity to ask questions or make comments and suggestions. Change is always embraced more readily if the reasons are understood and employees feel that they have had the chance to become involved in the process.

Show from your actions and attitude that you are positive and not apprehensive.

If changes are directed from someone in the hierarchy above you, by all means question the reasons for them, if you feel inclined to. But once the decision has been made, even if you don't fully agree, never voice your dissenting opinion down the line.

CHARACTER

I don't think there is a more inspiring definition than the one I heard used by Cavett Robert – made in front of a large audience in Kansas City.

He said…**"Character is the ability to carry out a good resolution long after the spirit in which it was made has disappeared".**

This one sentence has influenced me greatly and helped me accomplish many things I might otherwise not have done.

Were it not for that statement, now indelibly etched into my subconscious, you would not be reading this book. Writing it would still have been just "a good intention".

CHOICE

Without doubt this is your greatest power!

(If you have a strong religious faith you may say that the power of prayer is your greatest power and I wouldn't argue with that, but don't underestimate what follows.)

Choosing is something we are doing all the time.

Wherever you currently are in your adult life is a result of all the countless choices you have made.

We choose what we wear, what we eat, what we read, what we watch on television, what we listen to, how hard we work...

It's essential to realise and acknowledge that *we choose* what we say and how we say it… how we think and what we think about … what environment we expose ourselves to… who we associate with…

How we invest our time … how we spend our money … how much (or little) we save.

How much we eat…how much we drink…whether to smoke or not…to take some regular exercise or not.

To buy or not to buy. To borrow or not to borrow.

We choose between honesty and deceit. We choose between action and procrastination.

We choose our attitudes and our responses to all the issues that confront us every day.

The list is endless.

Every day we are faced with a huge number choices and decisions.

And the choices and decisions we make will be entirely consistent with our goals and our self-image.

There is no escaping the fact that the person you are, the life you are leading, the things you do, are almost entirely a result of the choices you have made in your life so far.

Read that sentence again.

Reflect on it. Be open-minded about it. Don't rationalise or try to make excuses.

You and I are where we are today primarily as a result of the choices we have made.

Now doesn't that give you incredible power to affect your future!

COACHING

There's a lot to be said for coaching and being coached. The difference between coaching and training is that coaching is more personal and is generally one to one, tailored to address specific needs and for achieving specific results.

If you can find somebody who is willing and able to assist you in acquiring certain skills you will find it can give you a real leap forward.

But here's a strong word of caution.

At the moment there's a fad called Life Coaching. And there are a lot of fakes out there, so you must be careful.

Life coaches are popping up everywhere.

There will of course be some genuinely good ones. But there are stacks of them who are preying on the vulnerable. Making promises that they can 'transform your life'. They use psychobabble and hackneyed phrases - such as 'empowering yourself' and 'letting go of your self-limiting beliefs'.

They all use the same language because they've all copied it!

If you check them out you'll find most have never succeeded at achieving anything worthwhile in their own lives. They've attended a few motivational seminars and then set up a business to tell others how to become happy and successful!

So if you are going to take advice about anything, as on occasion you should, check out the credentials of who you take it from first.

Don't listen to anybody who hasn't 'walked the walk'.

COMMITMENT

Having chosen your career and the company you work for (assuming you don't work for yourself of course), it deserves your total commitment.

If you are self employed you had better be utterly committed or you'll soon be looking for a job!

Your commitment should be total. Don't be disappointed if you don't always succeed in extracting the same amount of commitment from people who may report to you. Remember - you are now exceptional!

Those who make it to the top will be those who understand the need for commitment.

The same applies to achieving your goals.

COMMON SENSE

Common sense isn't always common practice, but common sense is worth far more than mere academic qualifications. I'm not knocking education – far from it. But as I've already pointed out 'the world is full of educated derelicts'.

Give me good plain common sense every time.

COMMUNICATION

When dealing with people it's essential that you develop good communication skills.

There are many ways that communication takes place, and it's taking place all the time!

In a large organisation it's vital that systems exist whereby all levels of management are "singing from the same hymn sheet".

People respond well to being "dealt in". They appreciate the opportunity to communicate their own thoughts and ideas. From time to time you should check how well the communication system in your organisation is working.

For those of you in senior management, or aspiring to reach it, you should frequently talk to employees who are working on the 'ground floor'. Find out what they think about the Company and its objectives etc. You may be in for a few shocks.

Communication between individuals is of paramount importance. The way you speak to people, the way you look at people, the way you listen to people, the way you write to people, what you say and how you say it, all have a significant impact. It's always worth getting feedback to make certain people understand what it is you are saying and trying to accomplish.

Since communication is a two-way thing, you should also ensure that you have an accurate perception of what is being communicated to you.

COMPOUND INTEREST

Put it into partnership with time and you have the greatest formula in the world for accumulating wealth! It will work for everyone! We'll cover this in more detail later.

CONCEIT

Beware as you progress in your career and in your life that you don't start to believe all your 'press clippings'. Don't forget how you got to where you are. There are few worse 'turn-offs' than an 'ego-tripper'.

CONCENTRATION

It's concentrated attention that gets things done.

A magnifying glass held still enough to focus the sun's rays on one spot would start a fire in a matter of minutes. Keep moving it about however and nothing happens!

Focus your attention on one job at a time. Work on increasing your attention span.

Establish the habit of finishing one task before starting another one. If a job is too long or demanding to be completed in one go, set a time that you will work until, or a stage you will reach.

CONSCIENCE

When all is said and done it's your own conscience you have to reckon with. There's no pleasure in achieving anything if you are troubled with your conscience over the way you did it.

It's essential to abide by "the golden rule", "Do unto others as you would have them do by you".

That's not saying don't be tough-minded. Being demanding, strong, pragmatic with high expectations of others is not just OK but a necessary quality of good leadership.

But that doesn't mean "wheeling and dealing", using people, being two-faced, deceitful or dishonest.

Make sure you can sleep easy!

COURAGE

It's not the absence of fear – it's the conquest of it!

John Wayne is quoted as describing courage as, "Being scared but saddling up anyway"

Sometimes we simply have to do things we are afraid to do.

I'm not suggesting you put yourself in mortal danger, but dealing with, and overcoming, fear is an essential part of growing.

A valuable self-motivator is to say to yourself, "Where there is nothing to lose by trying and everything to gain if successful by all means try… Do It Now!"

Next time you suffer from an irrational fear of attempting something try saying it.
It works! But it only works if you immediately act.
You must get into action as soon as you say those magic words "Do it now!"
By doing so you will be developing an exceedingly powerful habit which can enable you to overcome procrastination at will.

COMPENSATION

There is definitely a law of compensation.

Given enough time everybody gets what he or she deserves.
No doubt you are familiar with the saying "What goes around comes around".
I truly believe that eventually we get paid back for whatever we do.
Don't ask me how that works…I haven't a clue. But it seems to be one of those Universal Laws.
Many would call it Karma.

There have been times in my life when I've seen one or two people seemingly 'getting away with murder'. Even to the point that I had begun to wonder if there is indeed any justice in this world. But, without exception, eventually the 'chickens came home to roost'
So you should never forget that what you give is what you will get. You can depend on it!

CREATIVITY

There's always a better way! A new idea or perhaps an original solution to an old problem. Continually encourage creative thinking from yourself and others.

If it weren't for man's incredible creative ability we would still be living in caves.

You'll have noticed the Wright brothers didn't start out by developing an A380, and Henry Ford's first cars didn't have heaters and windscreen washers, or Bluetooth and air-conditioning!
Not even a Sat Nav!

Everything can continually be improved. Especially ourselves!

CREDIBILITY

You will only manage your relationships with people successfully whilst you have credibility. Once you lose that you're sunk.

Be yourself ... show that you are human. Don't try to act like you are infallible ... but at the same time you'd better know what you are talking about most of the time.
You'd better know how to do what you ask others to do – and demonstrate it from time to time ... and always be honest.

CRITICISM

The easiest thing in the world to dish out... and the toughest to take! Fight the urge to criticise. Constant criticism of others (even if only to yourself) demonstrates a lack of your own self-esteem.

Having said that, if you are responsible for the performances of others, it will of course become necessary to occasionally constructively criticise and appraise.
Do it in private. Always say something positive first. Be brief and to the point. Be specific. And show a sincere desire to help by suggesting how improvement can be achieved.

When you are on the receiving end of criticism be open minded enough to at least accept that it may be valid! Furthermore, if you hear the same criticism of yourself from more than one person you'd better start to sit up and take notice.
It comes hard to discover we aren't perfect all of the time!

CYNICISM

Don't be a cynic. It's a negative trait you could well do without. I'm convinced it's better to err on the side of naivety than to suspect a sinister motive behind everything.

D

DELEGATION

Learning to multiply yourself through others is going to be necessary in order to increase your own effectiveness and develop the skills of others. It's through 'doing' that people learn best.

SOME DON'TS

    a) Don't delegate all the jobs that you dislike doing and keep the perks for yourself.

    b) Don't delegate a task without giving the authority to carry it out.

    c) Don't constantly look over his/her shoulder.

    d) Don't try getting people to do things they haven't been taught how to do or have any guidelines for.

    e) Don't change what he/she did unless critical (in which case you probably made a bad decision as to what to delegate, or to who you delegated to, in the first place).

    f) Don't expect people to be as good at something as you are. You've probably had more practice – and you are where you are because you must have done some things well.

DO …

    a) Be specific

b) Be supportive

c) Select priorities

d) Delegate everything that can prevent you from doing the most important and effective things that only you should do.

DETAILS

Give them lots of attention. *It's often the little differences that make the big difference.* Don't get bogged down by the minutia but do realise that it's those extra concerns and touches that make for excellence.

DETERMINATION

When invited to speak at a very large meeting, Winston Churchill stood and addressed his audience for what probably still stands as a record for the shortest speech ever.

He stood up and waited until there was total silence as the assembled group eagerly awaited words of wisdom from this famous and inspiring leader. He then said the following: -

"Never, never, never give up!"

Upon which he sat down!

You can imagine the amazement of his audience at the brevity of his oratory!

The power of the message was made all the more apparent by the succinct way in which it was delivered.

It is undoubtedly the only speech ever made that every person who heard it was able to memorise and repeat verbatim!

It's obvious that Churchill considered 'determination' critical to success. A determined person is formidable indeed. **Your degree of success will certainly be proportional to your degree of resolve and your definiteness of purpose.**

DEVELOPMENT

Start with yourself. How are you planning to be more effective tomorrow than you are today? What is your programme to become more proficient, better educated, fitter and stronger – both physically and mentally?

Since you've read this far I'm going to assume that you are motivated to improve and develop yourself.

Hopefully these tips, techniques and principles will reveal ways in which you can encourage others to do the same. The development of production and profits within a business is very much related to the development of the people who work in it.

More importantly the quality of *your own* life will improve immeasurably if you are continually stretching yourself to grow.

DISCIPLINE

Perhaps I should have resisted including this until getting to the S's to use the heading 'Self Discipline'. But it simply wouldn't wait!

It's just so important. It is one of the key ingredients of THE SUCCESS SYSTEM

Of all the behavioural qualities that separate real achievers from the 'also rans', the most important is self-discipline.

Let's repeat that. ***Self-discipline is the single most important characteristic that separates winners from losers.***

One of the most profound statements of all time, certainly one that has positively affected thousands of lives, including mine, is as follows: - **"Successful people are those who have formed the habit of doing the things that failures don't like doing".**

Imagine how productive and successful you could really become if you would discipline yourself to follow through on all your good intentions.

Think for a moment about all those people who are massively overweight, or slowly killing themselves through smoking or drinking too heavily, those who loaf around in front of the TV hour after hour and night after night, people who spend everything they earn and spend all they can borrow. Millions will go to their graves having nothing to show for their time on this earth other than regret at knowing all that they could have done…but never did.

All because they sadly failed to develop sufficient self-discipline to take control of their lives.

Don't allow yourself to become one of them!

This is so fundamental to living your life to the full and fulfilling your potential we are going to come back to it again and again.

E

EFFECTIVENESS

Don't confuse effectiveness with efficiency. **Effectiveness is a measure of results**. In other words what has been achieved. It's much more important to be effective than efficient. Get the job done.

Efficiency is a measure of effort. If the effort is of little consequence then it's been wasted. Effectiveness is what counts. But if you can be efficient *and* effective so much the better.

It is no good discovering the most efficient way to do something – if it's not what you really should be doing.

EGO

There's nothing wrong with having an ego. We all do to a greater or lesser degree. Just make sure that your ego doesn't have you.

It's ego drive that compels people to action and creates the determination to excel. It's the genesis of a competitive spirit. It's wholesome and good, providing it's under control.

But there's nothing more likely to alienate people than 'big-headedness'.

Boastfulness, pushiness and vanity are definitely traits to avoid.

EMPATHY

I have no idea how to teach or impart the skill of demonstrating empathy. The ability to 'put yourself in another person's shoes' and see things from their point of view is something you'll only acquire if you really are concerned about other people, and not too wrapped up in yourself to bother about the feelings of others.

Empathy doesn't mean sympathy. Commiserating with somebody isn't necessarily going to do much to solve his or her problem. In fact it could possibly compound it.

But being able to objectively think through what you might do in a similar situation may be valuable indeed.

Don't fall into the trap of assuming you know what you would do, or feel, in situations that you've never experienced in your own life.
A wealthy person can easily empathise with somebody with very little money – if he or she started out with nothing. If, however, their wealth was inherited, there is no way he or she could possibly fully understand the anguish, frustration and misery of poverty.

There are situations that some people may find themselves in that would be impossible for you or me to begin to imagine. In those circumstances we can't empathise, but we can still offer support and encouragement where appropriate.

EMOTIONS

Happiness, sadness, fear, greed, envy, love, hate, anger, frustration, excitement...

We are all familiar with each of these feelings.

There's nothing wrong with that. That's what life is made up of.

Some of these emotions are brilliant – in the right place and at the right time.

But sometimes they can be harmful if allowed to get out of hand.

The key is to be able to keep them under control.

Emotions are not always subject to logic or reason. But they are always affected by action.

Try acting as if you are happy when you're feeling a bit down. Deliberately put a big smile on your face. Tell yourself out loud what a great day it is! Act as if you are really excited about something. Keep it up for ten minutes or more. I guarantee you will discover a real change in your mood.

Act as if you are full of confidence when you're not... and you'll become more confident!

Act enthusiastically…and you'll become enthusiastic!

Act happy…and you'll become happy!

Try it. It really works.
You'll be amazed at how you can learn to become a master of your own emotions!

ENERGY

Clearly energy is related to good exercise, getting sufficient sleep and sensible eating habits.
For many of us a brief catnap for twenty minutes around mid-day, or early afternoon, can produce a good energy boost.
But, most of all, energy seems to be related to the degree of one's motivation and is self-generating. Spend a lazy day doing nothing and see how tired you get! Conversely the more you have to do – the harder you work the more energy you'll seem to have.

ENTHUSIASM

The only thing more contagious than enthusiasm is the lack of it!

It doesn't mean ranting and raving – jumping up and down and waving your arms – but real enthusiasm will put a smile on your face, some passion in your voice and a light of conviction in your eyes that others will be captivated and affected by.

Enthusiasm has a mesmerising and magnetic quality. It's totally impossible not be energised when confronted by someone with genuine enthusiasm.

So put a spring in your step and some zest in your life!

Enthusiasm is the little difference that makes the big difference!

ENVIRONMENT

If you go to Tokyo you'll almost certainly notice that the children there speak Japanese!

There are a lot of Catholics in Italy. If you were born and raised in Newcastle it's probable you have a 'Geordie' accent.

Pretty obvious stuff.

We are all products of our environment.

Never underestimate the impact that the environment you've been exposed to so far in your life has had on you.
And the environment surrounding you today will continue to influence you. So be very careful about your choice of companions ... where you live and with whom you socialise ... what you listen to ... what you watch and what you read.

Just as what you take in through your mouth will affect your physical wellbeing for better or worse, so what you take in through your ears and your eyes will affect what and how you think and how you behave.

Make no mistake about this.

Recently I was the guest speaker at a conference and during my presentation I threw into the audience some horse chestnuts. I invited those who caught them to tell me what they were.

"Conkers" came back the unanimous reply. *Not a single person suggested that they were potential Horse Chestnut trees!*

In order to drive the point home I then showed them a packet of runner bean seeds that still had a few seeds left in it. The seeds were exactly the same as they had been several months earlier when the packet had been opened.

But some other seeds from that same packet, which had been planted at the top of my garden in rich soil, had rapidly become a thick mass of stems and leaves, towering well over six feet, and for several weeks had produced a daily crop of succulent runner beans.

Now the point of this is clear. Placed in the right environment, conducive to growth, a seed will flourish.

And the same thing is true of you and me!

Permit me to tell you a true story that profoundly illustrates how the environment to which we are exposed can have an incredible influence on what we can become.

Several years ago my wife Sue and I, together with our two boys, were invited to a lunch party to celebrate the 18th birthday of Mark, the son of some very good friends of ours. It was a really happy gathering of family and friends.

Needless to say there were plenty of cameras in action, as there usually are on these occasions.

What made this particularly amusing was the presence a beautiful little girl who insisted that she wanted to be in every photo! She had such an exuberant outgoing personality and was chock full of vitality, with a smile that simply captivated everyone.

She was a non-stop chatterbox, about five years old, with stunning jet-black hair and the most gorgeous brown eyes.

She was Chinese.

Looking around it was difficult to identify her parents, as there wasn't a Chinese adult to be seen.

But it didn't take long to figure out who she belonged to …they were the couple that kept trying to calm her down!

By now you will have realised that she had been adopted.

Fascinated, I struck up conversation with the adoptive parents who willingly told me the background of how and where they found her.

It wouldn't be appropriate, nor is it necessary, to go into great detail here. But it was an inspiring story. The crux of which is this.

At the time of adoption she was living in an orphanage in China. She was 18 months old.
She couldn't talk. She couldn't even walk.

You can imagine the overwhelming emotions we felt looking at this beautiful child who had an abundance of energy and enthusiasm who, had she not been rescued by this wonderful couple would, in all probability, have no longer been alive.

The loving and caring environment that they had provided for her had totally changed and transformed her life.

Now seeds have no control over where they fall and what happens to them.

And little children can't choose their environment either.

But you can! And must!

It's imperative to select a positive and wholesome environment – seek out and associate with achievers and doers.

If you mix with negative people and losers you are going to become just like them.

I'll say it again.

Never ever underestimate the importance of your environment.

EVALUATION

If you want people to grow you must evaluate their performance from time to time.

Don't tell everybody else how somebody is doing and forget to tell the one person who really needs to know.

It's truly amazing that often it takes a funeral to provoke people into expressing their love and their admiration for the departed. Trouble is, by then it's too late.

Wouldn't it be better to have told him or her how you felt while they were still alive and able to appreciate it?

So, if you are really pleased with the performance of an employee, or even one of your children come to that, for goodness sake let them know!

Equally if you are dissatisfied don't keep it a secret. How will they know if you don't tell them?

Just be sure to criticise in private. Naturally, nobody minds being praised in public.

EXAMPLE

Sooner or later if you have any leadership skills at all, the organisation you head up is going to reflect and resemble the example you set.

You'll hear your own anecdotes and pet sayings passed on down the line. Even your idiosyncrasies will stand a fair chance of being copied.

Also bear in mind that, if you are a parent of a young child, your standards and values will almost certainly be adopted.

So watch yourself – what you do and what you say – and how you do it and how you say it. When you stand in front of the mirror be sure you can live with the reflection.

EXCITEMENT

It's not just for little children anticipating a birthday or Christmas!

Even now I can still get excited at lots of things. In this world there is so much to be excited about. If your attitude is right!

The prospect of spring after a long winter…the start of a new Football Season.

Flying off on holiday…seeing my grandchildren…opening a bottle of great wine…the first barbecue of summer…going to the theatre…coming home after a business trip abroad…getting in a new car…firework displays…watching the sun come up…a snowstorm…walking on a beautiful beach…outdoor concerts…opening a present…the smell of freshly baked bread…the Chicago skyline…Sydney Harbour…a day on a boat…lunch in a country pub…Charlton scoring a goal!

That's just a very short list of the many things I can get easily excited about.

What's on your list? And what's on the list of things you would love to do but can't afford to at the moment?

Believe me…if you are prepared to follow and put into practice what I'm sharing with you, you'll achieve everything that you can think of, if the prospect of doing so excites you.

And also believe me when I tell you that there is something awesome about the "ability to achieve" when a group of people get excited about a mutually agreed objective. But how do you get others excited?

Get yourself excited first!

EXERCISE

It's impossible to over emphasise the benefits you will derive from taking regular exercise.

When I was in my mid thirties, my idea of exercise was to sit in a bath, pull out the plug, and fight the current!

Then I got caught up in the jogging craze that took hold when I was living in America.

Since getting into the habit of running for between 30 or 40 minutes, at least on two or three mornings a week, (I must admit that it's quite often a slow jog on a treadmill these days) I have become a total convert to the need to keep in reasonable physical shape.

Now I don't want to sound sanctimonious about this. I have never been thrilled about getting out of a warm bed to go to the gym, or to run in the open air on a dark, cold or wet morning; however I can truthfully say that, on every occasion after I do it, I feel great and am glad that I did.

It's not my intention – neither am I sufficiently qualified, to write a book on physical fitness. You can find plenty of good books on the subject in any High Street bookshop or on the internet, but I can testify to the benefits of physical fitness - you'll look better - feel better - have more energy, and have an improved self-image.

You will probably add years to your life also.

EXPECTATIONS

Strangely, most people will live up to your expectations – provided they know what they are.

They will also live *down* to your expectations! If you have a low opinion of someone it is seldom they will disappoint you.

Your children will provide convincing evidence of this.

The real problem here is that far too often management fails to really let people know specifically what is expected of them or how they are doing. "Work hard" or "do your best" is hardly specific and is certainly liable to a variety of interpretations. Let people know what you want from them – and have high expectations.

EXTRA-MILE EFFORT

These days good service is becoming a rarity, especially in the UK. Many people seem to act as if everything is too much trouble. They want to get away with doing the minimum amount of work possible.

How many times when calling a company (assuming you ever get to talk to a real person that is!) have you been pushed around from person to person?

Few people want to take the responsibility or make a genuine effort to assist you, so they just hand you over to someone else in another department. I'm sure you've had similar experiences.

So if you want to stand out as being exceptional it won't be difficult!

Doing just that little bit more can often make such a big difference. It needn't mean working longer hours – just doing more in the hours you do work. The extra sales call – that additional phone call. Going out of your way to give outstanding service to a customer. Exceeding expectations. Doing today what most people would put off until tomorrow. Develop that 'extra mile' habit and you will keep your star in the ascendancy.

F

FAILURE

Try not to make a habit of it! But nobody gets everything right every time either.

The occasional failure is good for the soul – it will keep your feet on the ground and should make you all the more determined to pick yourself up and get back in there.

Nobody should be ashamed of failure. People should be ashamed of giving up or not even trying.

FAIRNESS

There is no such thing.

If there was we would all have 'film star' good looks, be brilliantly musical, have fantastic singing voices, be superb athletes…

No need to go on. You get the picture. Life isn't always fair. Each of us has to make the most of what we have.

But you should at least strive to achieve fairness in every decision you make that affects other people.

FAITH

You'd better believe in something.

How about yourself, other people, your company and your products or services for starters?

Faith amounts to complete trust or confidence without logical proof. You'll need faith in order to genuinely visualise achieving your major definite goal, long before you actually realise it.

Faith is belief in an unseen and unknown power or influence working for your benefit. That's when you'll know you're being helped along the way.

It's the powerful extra 'dimension' that guarantees the final outcome.

FAMILIES

If you are responsible for employing people remember that most of them will have families so don't neglect thinking about their welfare, or the influence that families can have either.

As for our own families it's my belief that being part of a wonderful family is one of the greatest blessings anyone could ask for. Despite the occasional disagreements or arguments....and the cost!

FATIGUE

Fatigue makes cowards out of all of us. When we are tired it's much easier to get dejected, to give up, get depressed and see the worst.

Don't work yourself into the ground. Don't be a martyr. Take holidays and even long weekends from time to time. Get at least six hours sleep a night...seven or eight would be even better.

I like the story of the young golf pro who regularly caddied for some of the most successful business leaders who frequently played at one of the country's leading golf clubs.

One day he plucked up the courage to ask one of these 'captains of industry' how he found the time to play so often whilst being in charge of a huge multinational company.

"Son", came the reply, "if the job takes you past lunchtime then it's just too big for you!"

Now I'm just kidding of course, but there is a message there. Learn to work smarter, not harder.

Real achievers don't measure their success by the hours they put in. It's what you put into each of those hours that counts!

FAVOURITES

Be careful. It's human nature to like being with some people more than others. But at work you play favourites at your peril.

It won't take long for people to realise where they stand. You could end up losing a lot of good people – and keeping some dummies.

FAVOURS

It pays to be owed a few, rather than the other way around.

Always remember that there is a law of reciprocity in this world.

But do take on board that people like to do favours. So don't hesitate to ask if you really need one.

FEAR

Most people could achieve so much more in their lives if they could simply overcome their fear. It's a natural emotion designed to keep us safe. But it can be a very harmful emotion if it prevents us from trying.

In any worthwhile endeavour there will always be some degree of associated risk. You are unlikely to succeed at anything if you are scared to try. By all means you should make sure you understand the risks, and that you have a contingency plan to cope with the downside if things don't go the way you hoped or expected. But, as the saying goes 'nothing ventured nothing gained'.

Don't allow fear to become the barrier to you fulfilling your potential. Every successful and wealthy person has made mistakes and experienced some failures in their lives. But they aren't afraid to pick themselves up and keep going.

When you pluck up the courage to do what you are afraid to do, you will take a quantum leap towards achieving your lifetime ambitions.

Remember...fortune favours the brave!

FINANCIAL MATURITY

Spending less than you earn!

(We'll talk much more about this under the two headings **Money** and **Wealth**)

FORMULAS

Most things can be reduced to a formula. Get into a habit of looking for the principles that apply to success in what you or others do. Make a note of them. Remember them. Practice them.

Great chefs know that superb dishes are created from the right ingredients and the right recipe. It never changes; the results are always the same.

FUTURE

John Gale wrote, "If you don't think about the future, you won't have one."

That's another way of saying that if you aim at nothing you'll hit it every time.

But just thinking about your future isn't enough. You have to visualise your future.

You need to know where you are going. Even if right now you don't know how you are going to get there.

There is an undeniable magic that will come into play when you really start to focus on what you want and where you want to be.

Somehow you will start to harness all the resources and attract the opportunities you need to take you towards your goals.

G

GENEROSITY

If you hate parting with your money be careful, nobody likes a skinflint. You don't have to chuck it around either. There is a difference between meanness and prudence.

You certainly should be generous with your time and your encouragement where others are concerned. Don't however, be so over generous with your praise that it becomes gratuitous.

GOALS

They are essence of all motivation and achievement.

Man is a goal striving individual. Lack of achievement, typical of so many people, can be directly related to their lack of goals, or low goals, or poorly defined goals.

There is a world of difference between "I want to be rich" and "I intend to be worth more than three million pounds before I am fifty". (Just one million isn't really enough these days, is it?)

The subject of goal setting could well fill a book. In fact there have been many articles and books written that cover goal setting as the major theme.

I'm going to share the key elements with you here. Because it's absolutely crucial that you understand how to set and achieve goals – and also, if you are a manager, how to help others do likewise.

Now why is goal-setting so important?

In a study undertaken by Harvard University in 1979, graduates were asked how many of them had written goals with action plans for their achievement.

- 3 percent had clearly defined written goals.
- 13 percent had goals but hadn't written them down.
- 84 percent had no goals in any shape or form.

The follow up study of the same Harvard students took place in 1989 and revealed that over the ten year period **the three percent who had**

written their goals were ten times more successful than the ninety seven percent who had not.

This demonstrates beyond any doubt, that the power of setting and writing down personal goals is awesome!

Goals should be specific and measurable, at least to some degree.

All that is required is a pen, a pad of paper and some time on your own.

Before undertaking this exercise sit back, get yourself relaxed, and start to think about all the important aspects of your life as discussed under the heading 'Balance'.

To achieve all that you are capable of achieving, you must develop a clear sense of direction.

Try to picture in your mind where you want to be. Ask yourself the most important question of all: "What do I really want to do with my life?" Most people never specifically answer that question to themselves, which is why most of them fail to accomplish what they are truly capable of.

The ultimate goal is happiness.

For most of us the major factors in being happy are; health and fitness, loving relationships with our family and friends, fulfilling and satisfying work, financial freedom, and inner peace. When you have all these in abundance you will be genuinely happy most of the time. You will become happier just by moving towards the attainment of these ideals.

Goals have to be believable – if you can't visualise the attainment – if you can't actually "see it in your own imagination" you won't achieve it.

Goals should be challenging enough to excite and stimulate but not so high that they are unrealistic. Remember this little quote *"aim to go as far as you can see – and before you get there you'll always see a little further"*.

Think about your goals every day and review your progress with regularity. Break them into short-term and long-term.

Share them only with someone you trust and who will mentor you and encourage you.

Writing them down where you can read them regularly is really effective. Don't ask me why…trust me.
Read them out loud every morning.

Have a plan for achieving them – some of your longer term goals may be difficult to plan for precisely, but at least you must know where and how to get started.

And remember:

You will only ever achieve goals that are consistent with your own self-image.

You should set goals in five areas:

1. Personal goals.
2. Family and relationship goals.
3. Financial goals.
4. Business and career goals.
5. Health and fitness goals.

Don't be afraid to aim high.
Visualise yourself having achieved them. Set deadlines and timeframes.

If it's a new car that you want then know exactly what make and model, what colour, and what equipment you want.
Imagine yourself taking delivery.
If it's a new house that you want then decide, precisely as you possibly can, what it will look like. How many rooms? How big a garden? What kind of location?

The power of imagination is awesome. It will propel you towards the achievement of whatever you visualise.
It will ingrain deep into your sub-conscious mind and have a profound affect on your determination and belief.

Most of your actions are dictated by your sub-conscious. But your sub-conscious is programmed by your conscious mind. That's why it is so vital to feed it with the correct instructions!

As Earl Nightingale stated in his brilliant book 'The Strangest Secret'
"You become what you think about all day long"

Now, I stated earlier that you should only set goals that you can conceive of achieving. And to begin with, it's essential for you to truly believe that you can achieve the goals that you set.

But once you fully realise the power of goal setting, and have proved it to yourself many times, you will be ready to "reach for the stars"

Great achievers have learned to dream big dreams and to attempt the impossible.

Because everything is impossible – until somebody does it!

Whatever you do, don't sell yourself short on this. I've never met a high-flyer who didn't set goals.

Most people have read about goal setting or heard about it on training courses, and yet unbelievably, if you could do a survey and be sure of getting truthful answers, I guarantee that you will be hard pressed to find evidence of more than a handful who had the self discipline to actually put it into practice.

H

HABIT

It's almost forty years since I gave up smoking, but I still recall that whenever my telephone rang, I would reach for my cigarettes and lighter before picking up the receiver.

As everybody who has ever smoked knows – smoking is not only exceedingly addictive – it's a habit – and a powerful one at that.

People didn't conveniently call me just at the precise moment when I needed a cigarette. It was purely through habit that I always smoked when answering the telephone.

We are all creatures of habit. If you are male I'll bet you always shave the same way. If you are a female and wear lipstick, in all probability you apply it in exactly the same way each time you put it on.

This undeniable tendency we have to acquire and follow patterns of behaviour is enormously powerful. But, as is the case with most forms of power, it can work for us or against us.

I'm so glad that I kicked the habit of smoking. It's wonderful not to smoke. I used to think I enjoyed smoking, but I enjoy not smoking a hundred times more!

Good habits can make you – bad habits can destroy you.

Think about that for a moment. Some habits are irritating to others, such as some speech habits – repeating the same phrase, e.g. "the fact of the matter is." or "I mean" before every sentence. Or "to tell you the truth" or finishing a sentence with "you know". Repeatedly saying "er" every few words.

Loudly clearing one's throat constantly is another irritating habit Check yourself, or ask someone to be candid with you, to see if you practise any of these, or any other irritating habits. Gum chewing is irritating to many people. Chewing on a wooden toothpick is a particularly unpleasant habit in some parts of America.

Make certain that you haven't acquired any habits that may cause people to dislike being around you. Don't hesitate to discreetly (and tactfully) tell others about habits that they may have, which are less than endearing.

Now let's look at some really harmful habits.

Procrastination!
Go back and read the section on Action!

Putting things off is one of the most destructive habits known to mankind!

Obviously there are some other seriously bad habits which are bound to cause you to fail, – cheating, lying, stealing etc. Sadly, for some people though, that's what they have become – habits.

How do you change bad habits? By replacing them with good ones!

In order to stop smoking and to stay committed, I took the money every day that I would normally have spent on cigarettes and put it in a jar. Seeing the amount start to quickly accumulate, as I regularly dropped the coins in, soon became an important factor in keeping me from the temptation to buy cigarettes. I had replaced the habit of smoking with a habit of saving!

If you are overweight get in the habit of refusing dessert. Or saying no to 'second helpings'. Change where you normally go for lunch and go for a walk instead. Eat an apple or some other low calorie snack. Get into the habit of regularly exercising.

There is a phrase I heard once which has stayed with me ever since. It's profound and worth remembering. Here it is.

'Motivation gets you started – habit keeps you going!'

It only takes a few weeks of repeating an action each day before it ceases to require much in the way of self-discipline. It will soon simply fit in to your way of life.

When managing people you will achieve miracles if you can structure things in a way that can ensure your people (and you too) acquire the correct work habits.

HEALTH

Almost everybody would put good health at the top of their list of things they want most.
Amazing then isn't it, how so many people seem so keen to put it at severe risk!

Smoking... overeating... too much alcohol... no exercise.

Isn't it odd that some people take more care of their car than they do their own body!

If you are a smoker let me assure you that I understand how addictive it can be. I smoked heavily from my late teens until I was in my early thirties. Quitting was fairly difficult...but only for a few weeks. Not a very high price to pay to reap all the benefits of being free from this appallingly destructive habit.

Now I'm not going to rehearse all the arguments as to why you must immediately give up smoking. You've heard them all many times.

On second thoughts it may be worth reminding you of some of the consequences. Smoking is a major cause of Heart attacks, Strokes, Emphysema and Lung Cancer. As if that isn't enough, an acquaintance of mine, a top Urologist in a London teaching hospital, recently catalogued for me a list of other lesser known but equally lethal conditions caused by smoking including Bladder Cancer.

Hopefully you realise that smoking makes your clothes and your hair smell which is most unpleasant for people around you. It will also make you look far older than you are by the time you reach your fifties.
    I realise if you are only in your twenties, that it's difficult to think twenty or thirty years ahead, it's the same issue with saving money for when you retire; but if you don't take action now eventually it will be too late. There can be no going back to put things right. A fatal Heart attack will take all the fun out of life.
    You know in your heart that you must stop. Not soon, or next week or whenever. Now!! Don't try to rationalise, just do it.

The same discipline applies to diet.
    The first time I remember seeing horrendously obese people was when I first went to the USA in 1970. At that time it was uncommon to see hugely overweight people in England. Sadly that's no longer the case. We have adopted similar eating habits and now junk food is almost as popular here as it is in America.
    We've arrived at a situation where there is a real likelihood that the present generation of young children will have a life expectancy shorter than that of their parents.

There is little point in going into great detail about what you should do if you are overweight. You are already fully aware of the need to stop eating rubbish.
    Don't make excuses about not having time to cook properly. It doesn't take much effort to prepare and cook fresh food. Fresh salads, fresh fruit and fresh vegetables are also a lot less expensive than most processed foods, and a lot healthier.
    Once more it all comes back to self discipline and good habits.

Here is an easy to follow weight loss plan that will work wonders for you:

Eat less. Exercise more.

There is another issue about health that I want to discuss and I realise it may be somewhat controversial. Certainly I have no wish to cause offence and I admit that I have no specific medical evidence to back up what I'm about to say. But it's based on years of observation and one particular personal experience with someone I knew really well. I can't go into more detail as I'm sure you will understand.

My belief is that many illnesses and ailments are psychosomatic in origin.

That doesn't mean that people only imagine they are ill; far from it. The condition, whatever it may be, will be real in most cases.

The point is however, that negative thinking people seem to get sick far more frequently than positive thinking people.

There are of course exceptions and I would be the first to acknowledge that fact, but trust me, this somewhat contentious statement is not being made lightly or recklessly.

Although I could give you many specific examples it isn't appropriate to do so here, but it may be worth mentioning that W.Clement Stone, who practised and preached the power of positive thinking, lived to be a hundred years old, and incredibly so did his wife Jessie. Hardly a coincidence I think!

Please believe me; your chances of enjoying continual good health will be greatly increased by looking after your body and adopting and practising a positive mental attitude with enthusiasm and passion in everything you do.

What a coincidence! Just as I finished writing the above I took a break to check my emails and on the home page of my browser was the following headline:-

'Don't Worry Be Happy': happiness is key to longer life.

I've copied the headline exactly as it appeared. As it was a fairly long article I'm only going to reproduce a few of the statements, but I'm delighted with the perfect timing of its publication as I freely admit to having been somewhat reluctant to discuss such a sensitive subject without any specific evidence to support my belief.

The following is a brief extract:

New research shows being happy can add several years to life. "Happiness does not heal, but happiness protects against falling ill" says Ruut Veenhoven of Rotterdam's Erasmus University in a study to be published next month.

After reviewing 30 studies carried out worldwide over periods ranging from one to 60 years, the Dutch professor said the effects of happiness

on longevity were "comparable to that of smoking or not"
That special flair for feeling good, he said could lengthen life by between 7.5 and 10 years.

Happy people were more inclined to watch their weight, were more perceptive of symptoms of illness, tended to be more moderate with smoking and drinking and generally lived healthier lives.
They were also more active, more open to the world, more self-confident, made better choices and built more social networks.

Among healthy populations happiness appeared to protect against falling ill, thus prolonging life.
My conviction has been vindicated!

HIDDEN STRENGTHS

Before you criticise anybody please remember this.

Hidden strengths are brought out by good finding, not by fault finding.

The more good you find in others the more good you will see in yourself.
The opposite is also true.

HOLIDAYS

Take them. Enjoy them. If you feel you can't leave your job for a couple of weeks then you're a lousy manager or businessperson.

I always found that, provided I gave enough lead in time, my people always did brilliantly when I was away. They were determined to show me I wasn't needed!
Make sure that all your people take their holidays too.

HONESTY

The truth always has the ring of truth about it!

Remember – life keeps books on us all. So if you can't think of any better reason than simply being able to sleep at night – you'll find life is easier, less complicated and eventually far more rewarding, if you make honesty your policy in all your dealings with people.

It sometimes takes courage to be honest and to tell the truth. But remember, you should always do the right thing. Because it's the right thing to do.

HUMOUR

It's not necessary to be a 'duty comedian' or try to be the 'life and soul' of every party, in fact you shouldn't be – **but everyone loves a sense of humour.**

Being able to laugh – especially at ourselves – and see the funny side of things, is a really desirable quality.

Of course, there is time to be serious and a time to have fun – the two shouldn't be confused. But no job is so important that you and your colleagues shouldn't have fun and enjoy what you are doing.

Here's a little warning – if you aren't good at telling jokes – don't tell them! If you have to wonder if a particular joke is OK to tell in mixed company, it isn't.

There's little that's more excruciating than hearing good jokes told badly, and little that will demean you more emphatically than telling bad taste jokes.

I

IDEAS

How many brilliant ideas have you had? What did you do about them?

Ideas are ten a penny. *The person who puts them into action is priceless.*

Even your greatest idea will eventually die if subjected to indifference, apathy and low expectations.

INITIATIVE

I have no idea how you can develop this in others but it's a fact that far too many companies and poor managers do everything they can to stifle it. That's a great way to drive away all the talent in a company and keep all the mediocre "take no chances" muppets!

Encourage people to use their initiative. You will have a few accidents but you'll all grow a lot faster.

INTUITION

It seems that on nearly every occasion I've ignored my intuition I've regretted it.

You can't teach people intuition. Some people have that "extra sense" in abundance.

Women tend to be more intuitive than men.

I'm not suggesting that you should abandon logic and facts.

Continue to exercise good disciplines when making decisions. Don't start making every decision an emotional one.

What I am saying though – particularly where decisions involving people are concerned – is don't dismiss that nagging doubt or that 'gut feeling' either. It could be your greatest asset.

It's OK to gamble once in a while also. Provided the consequences of a mistake are not going to be dire!

Many people who have been promoted as a result of somebody's gut feeling, as opposed to 'being ready', have excelled beyond expectations.

If you are not particularly intuitive about people you could seek the opinion of somebody you consider having good intuitive ability.

INSPECTION

'Remove the fear of detection and punishment and you will create great instability within the individual'.

Sorry, I'm not sure of the source of that quote but I think it was Winston Churchill again.

Simply explained it means people need to know where the lines are drawn and what is permissible and what isn't.

It's a sad indictment on today's society in the UK that so much petty crime is committed on an unprecedented scale. During the two months before each Christmas it's estimated that over £500,000,000 worth of goods is stolen by shoplifters. Yes...that's five hundred million pounds! Many shoplifters don't get prosecuted and those that do invariably get off with a caution or a few hours of community service. Consequently, although detection rates are high, the punishment is often so derisory that there is very little deterrent. Perhaps if mandatory prison sentences were to be imposed for shoplifting the number of offences would reduce dramatically.

So if you run a business, or part of a business, don't allow your employees to be faced with temptation through your lack of vigilance, or you may be responsible for turning an otherwise decent person into a thief.

Don't foster a culture of snoops, tell-tales, special policemen or a KGB, but do check up on all your people from time to time; sometimes unexpectedly. Let them know that you do, and let them know that you did; either with praise for what you saw, or with a reprimand for what you didn't see.

You should never expect what you don't inspect.

INSPIRATION

Inspired people get inspiring results.

I have always believed that people have to motivate themselves.

Basically that's absolutely true; but people's ability to motivate themselves can depend on many external influences, and we will discuss that later when we come to motivation.
    Learning to motivate oneself at will is a skill that can be learned.
    Exposure to inspirational influences is one of the foremost factors.

There's inspiration to be found in a million places and in a million different ways.
    Music has, throughout the centuries, been able to stir men's blood and touch the emotions in an incredible way. Both in peace and in war.
    Great works of art. Little children. A newborn baby. Watching a skilled performer...a dancer... an athlete...a musician... a gifted soccer player.

I still remember the times when I was mesmerised by players like Jimmy Greaves and George Best.

(That dates me a bit!)

Watching those players display their exquisite artistry with a football was inspiring and magical and awesome to behold, and today the likes of Cristiano Ronaldo, Robin van Persie and Wayne Rooney possess skills that are simply breathtaking!

Outstanding works of literature. Majestic architecture – it may be as old and elaborate as the Palace of Westminster and Houses of Parliament, or St. Paul's Cathedral in London, or the bridges in Venice. Maybe even the modern elegance of the skyscrapers in Singapore or Chicago.

A tropical beach, a spectacular sunset, a spring morning.

The countryside after a snowstorm.

The unsung heroes who work unselfishly in deprived areas of the third world; having devoted their lives to the relief of starvation and despair.

A huge passenger plane taking off. (What a pity we can no longer enjoy magnificent Concorde).

The wonderful voice of the late Luciano Pavarotti.

The sound of a Welsh male voice choir. Thunderstorms that light up the sky.

These are just a few of the things that can thrill and inspire me. (Forgive me if I have repeated some of the things that I told you excited me. It's sometimes difficult to make the distinction between inspiration and excitement.)

How about you? Never be embarrassed to look for inspiration – to indulge in it, and to respond to it

It's only through individuals who have been inspired, and then acted, that this truly incredible planet of ours has moved from the Stone Age to the age of marvels and miracles in which we now live.

INTEREST (Compound)

Partner it up with time, as Rothschild once said, and you have the eighth wonder of the world!

(By interest I'm referring to the annual return on investment including dividends)

Read the following. (Taken from the Motley Fool) and be prepared to be amazed!!

The Magic of Time & Compound Interest*

Ann, a young woman of 20, decides to save £100 a month from her salary. She puts this into an investment plan, which gives her an average return of 14 per cent a year on her money. She contributes throughout her twenties whilst still enjoying everyday pleasures. At the age of 30 she meets Andrew – who has frittered away his twenties – and saved nothing. Nevertheless they set up home together and decide to have children. Ann stops working to bring up her young family – and stops contributing to her investment plan, Andrew however, who is the same age as Ann, now takes his responsibilities more seriously and starts to contribute £100 per month into a similar plan of his own, something which he continues until the age of 60.

The numbers look like this:

	Ann (£100 per month from age 20-30)	Andrew (£100 per month from age 30-60)
Age 20	0	0
30	26,453	0
40	98,069	26,453
50	363,562	124,522
60	1,347,806	488,084

Amazing isn't it? By the age of 60 Ann is still almost three times ahead of Andrew, although she has not contributed anything for thirty years!

*Taken from 'The Motley Fool'

Now you may be thinking that 14% is a bit unrealistic. In today's market that may look high. However if you take the average from the beginning of the 60's to the beginning of the 2000's it is very indicative of growth over that time. Remember, in some years the market can drop by more than 20 percent, but recovery always occurs soon afterwards. Also take into account that if in the future returns are lower, inflation will be lower too.

Just to use some different assumptions: if Ann had been saving £150 a month for ten years at an annual investment return of 11% and Andrew had also saved £150 a month but for 30 years having started ten years after Ann, also at an annual return of 11%, the result would be:- Ann at age 60 would have £750,500 and Andrew at age 60, having put away three times as much, would have £393,560.

Regardless of the rate of return, important as it is, you will readily recognise that it's the principle of combining Time and Compound interest that is really the important factor!

Since this book is aimed primarily at those who are aspiring to move ahead, I assume you probably fall into the age group of somewhere between 23-40. There is no reason why you should not become independently wealthy. **But you must start now!**

If however your 40th birthday is now just a memory please don't despair. It's never too late. Colonel Sanders the founder of Kentucky Fried Chicken was well into his sixties before he developed his famous recipe and found someone to bankroll his idea!

We are going to go into much more detail under the two headings **Money** and **Wealth**. I just wanted to give you a wakeup call and show you how anybody can eventually accumulate considerable wealth. The magic of **Time and Compound Interest** is the golden rule that every wealthy individual, who started with little or nothing, understands and uses.

INSURANCE

Having been involved in the selling and marketing of insurance for over thirty years, it's safe to assume that I am a passionate believer in the benefits of insurance protection.

Life insurance, health insurance, fire insurance, car insurance, accident insurance, travel insurance. I've owned plenty and I've sold plenty.

But the kind of insurance I believe in more that any other is self-insurance.

Everyone should expect the unexpected.

So how well prepared are you for those events you may not be able to foresee? What new skills are you learning? Are your affairs in order? How well would you react or adapt to a crisis in your life?

The broader your horizons the more "insurance" you'll have to face the challenges that life will confront you with from time to time.

INTEGRITY

Regardless of circumstances never ever prostitute your own integrity.

If you have to lie or cheat, or deceive, or renege on promises or deals, you're a failure.

No matter what position you now hold, no matter what material wealth you now possess, you are an abject failure.

And sooner or later everyone will know it.

For as I've already said, life keeps books on us all.

Don't ever ask or expect others to do anything that would be in conflict with their own integrity. Don't do business with people whose integrity is in doubt. Don't work for any organisation that may encourage you to be anything but totally honest.

Just like in those cowboy films we used to love as a kid... in the end it's the good guys who always win.

INTENTIONS

You'll realise how easy it is to succeed in this world when you consider this; *for most people good intentions remain just that.* They seldom translate those intentions into action.

We are all familiar with the saying 'the road to hell is paved with good intentions'.

The inability to overcome inertia and get into action is why most people go through their lives achieving next to nothing.

I'm told on good authority that every year during January, health clubs recruit more new members than in all the other months in the year put together. By March many of these new members have stopped going!

Also at the start of every year, we are inundated with advertisements for nicotine patches targeted at the thousands who have resolved to quit smoking. Within a couple of weeks most of those resolutions have already been broken.

Recently somebody told me about some interesting research conducted by the well-known company that markets language courses. Although I can't vouch for the authenticity of this information, based on the responses I've had when mentioning this to other people, I'm confident that it is pretty accurate.

Apparently, of all the language courses that are bought, more than fifty percent are never taken out of the cellophane wrapper!

Of those that are started, less than ten percent of the purchasers ever get as far as the last DVD or CD.

Doesn't this say it all?

If you will determine to translate your good intentions into action, and have the self-discipline to stay focused, you will outperform more than 90 percent of your fellow human beings!

INERTIA

Learn to overcome it! Do it now!!!

INVESTMENT

I'm so glad that you are investing your time by reading this book. The best investments you will ever make are those you make in yourself. Continue to do so and you'll be well rewarded.

In addition to investing in your ongoing education and development, investing part of what you earn is fundamental to your long term future if you want to live a life of abundance and freedom from financial hardship.

There are two headings later in this **A** to **Z** that specifically cover the acquisition and accumulation of wealth. They are: **Money** and **Wealth**. What's covered under these headings will have a massive impact on your financial future......if you are prepared to pay the price and follow the advice. I did and I'll be forever grateful.

IMAGINATION

Without the marvellous ability that man has to use his imagination, we would still be living in trees and caves!

Look around you at all the man made things you can see right now. Note the pattern of the material on the walls – the floor covering – the design of the furniture – the style of the curtains – the pictures on the wall – the clothes you are wearing – the shape of the building you are in. Your mobile phone or your computer. Your television or home entertainment system. Look outside the window. What else can you see that man has designed and manufactured? None of this would exist if somebody hadn't first visualised the outcome in his or her mind.

The power of the imagination is awesome. (OK, I know I said it earlier)

Everything that you and I now take for granted had to first exist in somebody's imagination before it could become a reality. Yet we often laugh at people with 'wild ideas' or vivid imaginations'. We tell children to 'stop being silly' when they play 'make believe' games. Imagination is the fundamental difference between us and every other living species!

Why make such a big deal of this? I'll tell you why.

Firstly, as already mentioned under the heading of creativity – nothing will change without creative people. The world depends on those who can apply creative thinking through the use of a fertile imagination. It's only then that things move forward and improve.

Look at today's cars, look at today's aeroplanes. Keyhole surgery, iPhones and iPads, digital cameras, and High Definition television.

Things these days improve by leaps and bounds. Technical advancement is taking place at a pace never known before in our history – all as a result of people who can imagine.

But there is a second and even more important reason that I am stressing this.

The nervous system has no way of distinguishing between a real experience and an imagined one!

Yes, it's a fact! Think about it for a while. Did you ever 'make-up' a few stories as a child? Chances are you did, of course, and if you told them enough times you started to believe them yourself. Remember?

The same is true for you now as an adult, as it was when you were a young girl or boy.

Hypnotism is a perfect example of this.

Now I'm not suggesting that you go around fabricating stories about yourself and your achievements in order to impress people. Far be it from that. But what I want you to consider is this. What you are today is a sum total of many things.

Heredity plays a part. Admittedly some gifts or talents – such as musical genius or a fine singing voice, were possibly bestowed at birth. But mostly we are who we are because of all the experiences we have had, and the influences of our environment. All this goes to form our 'self-image' – the way we see ourselves.

We will never differ from the way we see ourselves – it's a self-fulfilling destiny.

All our actions, decisions, choices will be compatible with our self-image.

But we can change our self-image!

If you start to 'see' yourself differently you will gradually change in order to become the person you now begin to see yourself as.

Please don't confuse that with 'wishing'. It's not the same thing at all. Wishing is the opposite. In most cases it's an admission of what's not likely to be, rather than what will be. A person *wishing* to be rich doesn't really expect it to happen.

But a person who 'sees' himself one day as being rich is much more likely to succeed in attaining wealth, as long as he can hold the picture in his mind and believe it to be true.

Cast your mind back to the last Olympic Games. If you were able to interview all those outstanding champions, most would admit to having 'dreamed of winning the gold medal'. Many openly admitted as much and said they had actually 'seen themselves' being presented with the gold medal. As if it had already happened!

Chris Hoy's mother, when being interviewed just after her son had won his third Gold Medal at the Beijing Olympics in 2008 (making him the first Briton in a hundred years to win three gold medals at the same games) told the reporter that he wrote in his diary when he was only thirteen that he would win an Olympic medal!

He won more in London four years later!

The power of imagination to drive us towards our goals is simply beyond belief.

As I told you earlier, one of the most revealing books I have read, – and one that explains so much about human behaviour, is 'Psycho-cybernetics' by Dr Maxwell Maltz. Don't be put off by the title. It's easy to read and has scores of examples of just how important and powerful our self-image is and how we can work to constantly improve it.

Watch a professional golfer when he's on the green – before making an important putt he'll take several practice shots, without actually touching the ball. What's he doing? That's right! He's imagining the ball rolling along the green and dropping into the hole.

The more vividly he can imagine it, the more likely it is to happen.

Dart players and snooker players do the same thing.

So dream a little. Start seeing yourself now as the person you want to become. Imagine in detail the kind of house you want to live in, or the car you want to drive. Imagine yourself in it. Know that it's going to be yours.

Hold clear pictures like these in your mind for a long time; regularly. Practice doing it when you're alone. If you run or jog or take walks, lose yourself in your thoughts and given free rein to your imagination. You will be fascinated and excited at just how creative and imaginative you really are.

IMPATIENCE

I've come to realise that impatience is a childhood trait, which, upon reaching maturity, should be controlled and even replaced, by patience.

Many years ago, when I bought my first house, the garden looked like a wilderness. At the time I couldn't get enthusiastic about doing much about it because I didn't have the patience to invest a lot of effort in doing something today that wasn't going to pay off by tomorrow – literally. Plants and shrubs and bulbs take months to grow!

I mention gardens in particular because they are so illustrative of the value of eventually reaping the benefit of efforts made much earlier.

Whenever my wife and I walk around our garden, we get immense pleasure and enjoyment from seeing how good it looks, whatever the time of year.

Since moving to our house, which had been newly built, we have transformed over an acre of mud, bricks and rubble, kindly left by the builders, to an expanse of garden vibrant with mature trees, shrubs, lawns, and flower beds, teeming with wonderful wildlife. There's also a big pond with hundreds of fish, visited in the summer by hordes of colourful dragonflies and butterflies

But it took time and sustained effort.

So much of our world today revolves around instant pay-off or gratification. In fact we are constantly being seduced into 'enjoying now and paying later'.

This philosophy may have some plusses – there's nothing wrong with the sensible use of credit – but it shouldn't become a total way of life.

Some things have to be paid for in advance, and often slowly, over time.

Saving and investing a minimum of ten percent of everything you earn is an infallible way of accumulating wealth. But you won't get rich after just a couple of years.

Losing a couple of stone, if overweight, can't be done in a day (amputating a leg may produce rapid weight loss, but won't solve obesity, or improve mobility!)

The same applies to getting fit. It takes time and effort.

Some things simply require patience and persistence.

This is especially true where people are concerned. Not everybody can learn fast or develop new skills rapidly – or change their way of doing things or change the way they think overnight. It takes time! So look for the gradual improvement. In other people as well as yourself.

Encourage it! Nurture it! Keep working at it! And you will see your patience pay off.

J

JOKES

Unless you tell them really well…don't. Better to listen to those who can.

This will never be more important than when speaking to an audience. Forgive me for saying again that if you ever wonder whether a particular joke can be told without offending anyone – don't tell it.

The best time to laugh at a joke is when it's on you!

JUDGEMENT

If you are not sure of your own, and the issue is important, seek the counsel of someone who is known to exercise his or hers wisely.

Nobody is right all the time either. So you can expect to get it wrong once in a while.

Don't pass judgement unless you have checked out all the facts.

And don't make hasty judgements either. Appearances can be deceptive.

JUSTICE

You can only do your best to do it or deliver it. It's a bit like fairness. There is probably no such thing as absolute fairness or justice.

But strive to be as scrupulous as possible if dispensing it.

Be very careful not to perpetrate a deliberate injustice. If you do, you will almost certainly never be forgiven.

If you've ever suffered an injustice you'll know exactly what I mean!

K

KEEPING QUIET

Don't, if to do so would prostitute your integrity.

Don't, if your only reason is to avoid confrontation at the cost of your conviction.

Do, if you are supposed to be listening!

When selling (and we all attempt to sell regularly) **always** keep quiet after having asked for the sale until the other person speaks.

KNOWLEDGE

Knowledge is power. *But only when it's used.*

Knowledge is of little or no consequence if it isn't backed by action.
  Having said that, it's imperative that you constantly strive to improve your knowledge in every way you can.

There are dozens of ways: Books, seminars, training courses, downloaded audio learning courses, evening classes, newspaper and magazine articles, private tuition, being coached or mentored...etc.etc.

If you truly intend to become successful there is a price to pay. That is to learn, learn some more and keep on learning. And put that knowledge into action!

L

LESSONS

We have all learned plenty of lessons during our lives. Sometimes the hard way.
  Better, and less costly if you can learn them from others. Otherwise,

as you know, engineers would have to re-invent the wheel every generation.

LEISURE

Don't feel guilty – enjoy it!

Hopefully, you enjoy your job and the work you do. But you should be working to live – not living to work.

In large companies there are nearly always people who are reluctant to take holidays. They cram their bags full of work to take home and hate to be anything but last out of the office each evening.
    Either they are fools, or so insecure that they are terrified somebody may 'steal a march on them'.
    For my money, it's the quality of the performance rather than the quantity of hours that impresses.
We aren't talking laziness here. Active leisure revitalises you.

Loafing about in front of a television, or surfing the internet for hour upon hour is not active leisure!
        Playing golf…playing tennis… swimming… cycling… gardening… sailing… playing football… playing cricket.
        Painting… drawing…photography…climbing…there's a multitude of things you can enjoy doing.

Leisure is vital to your health and sense of well-being.

For those with families, especially young children, spending time together is one of the most rewarding things you can do.

LEARNING

There's a lot to be said for having a good education.
    But don't be in awe of the highly educated – after all, we've all met some well educated morons.

Education doesn't count for much without common sense and is certainly useless without action.
    Nevertheless, it is incumbent on us all to keep learning throughout our careers and lives.

The fact you are reading this would indicate your agreement.

In addition to books, magazine articles and seminars, I have become a devotee of audio learning.

Considering the huge amount of time most of us spend in our cars, occasionally playing some learning CD's or downloads can easily turn 'driving time' into 'learning time'.

When I was young my father, who as you may recall was a lorry driver, would occasionally be called upon to chauffeur the company directors if the regular chauffeur was away for some reason. He used to consider this a great honour. I never mentioned it to my dad, but I used to consider it a great extravagance and indulgence.

On reflection, I now understand the benefits that business executives derive from utilising their time by reading or catching up on phone calls and emails, rather than just sitting behind a steering wheel staring at the number plate of the vehicle in front.

Today we don't need to go to the expense of hiring a chauffeur to put some of those hours spent travelling to valuable use. The iPod (with a Bluetooth connection) or CD player has enabled us to turn our vehicles into little schools on wheels.

There's an abundance of outstanding audio learning programmes available today.

In a matter of months you could learn a whole new language just driving to work!

LISTENING

An art to be mastered!

If you are anything like most people you probably much prefer to talk than to listen.

And when courtesy forces you to stop for a moment, rather than really listening to the other person, it's likely you're thinking about what you are going to say next!

Yet the wisest people I've ever met seem to do more listening than talking!

When they do talk – it's worth hearing what they have to say.

When we listen – we learn.

The need to talk and dominate the conversation is often a symptom of a desire to make a good impression.

But people are often more impressed by good listeners than good talkers.

Good listeners pay attention to people, they show interest and ask questions.

They make others feel important.

To hear does not always imply attention, but to listen always does.

Work at it.

LEADERSHIP

There have been many attempts to define it and to understand it.

I'm not entirely sure I can do proper justice to giving an accurate definition, but I do know what leaders are. They are those individuals who rise up from out of the crowd and take charge ... by consent.

There is no stereotype. They come in all shapes and sizes. They come from both sexes. They come from all nationalities.

Regardless of each leader's uniqueness and individuality – certain characteristics and qualities would seem to be common to all great leaders.

Here are some of the key ingredients.

Competence in your chosen career or profession. Competence is what we are talking about here... not necessarily genius. In team sports, like soccer for example, the player designated Captain isn't always the most skilful in the team. But he must be a competent player.

Leaders are never passengers.

Courage To go first
　　　　　　Of your convictions
　　　　　　To admit your mistakes
　　　　　　To stick your neck out
　　　　　　To take calculated risks

Charisma - that magnetic quality that gives off such positive vibes that people are literally drawn towards you.

Pioneering spirit - the urge to go to new heights and into new territory.

Being creative and innovative. Having and sharing a vision of a better tomorrow.

Emotional maturity - A great leader controls his or her ego rather than allow it to control him or her. He or she is not given to temper or tantrum.

Standards – Great leaders impose high standards of performance and behaviour on themselves and live up to those standards.

Self-discipline – Nobody lacking this quality would ever be considered a leader of any note.

Do not confuse leadership and management. There's a world of difference.
   Management, to some degree, can be defined as the operating of a system and the adherence to pre-determined procedures.
We are surrounded by that kind of management in many familiar situations.

>   Supermarket manager
>   Hotel manager
>   Office manager
>   Restaurant manager

I have no wish to be demeaning to people in those jobs. The point I would make though, is that these jobs, especially when part of a nationwide network of shops and supermarkets or hotels, carry little requirement for flair or expression or individuality.

That's not to say that good people skills aren't an asset. Those that demonstrate them will quickly rise in the ranks of the organisation.

The success of these companies, as with many franchises also, depends on the close adherence to a prescribed and proven system.

Leadership is for those of you who are willing to look for the thrill of marshalling the efforts and capturing the hearts and minds of others. Demonstrating the ability to inspire people into action. Being able to bring people together as a team, united in the quest for achieving a mutually agreed objective.

Leadership exists when others willingly, and even gratefully, follow.

Great leaders don't tell what to do.....they show how it's done.

LUCK

When you see people who seem to have everything going for them...a great job...a nice house...a dream car...and plenty of money, you may think that the world is sometimes a bit unfair.

How did they get so lucky?

One thing of which you can be almost certain is that they got into action – and they stayed in action.
    The amount of good luck that comes your way depends on your willingness to act.

One of the world's greatest golfers Arnold Palmer, (or perhaps it was Gary Player?), reportedly said when asked how he seemed to be so lucky, "It's amazing, but the more I practice the luckier I seem to get!"
    That just about sums it up.

Recently I read of a study that had been carried out over the past decade by Dr. Richard Wiseman on the subject of luck.
    The research concluded there was no such thing as good fortune.
    The study reveals that those with charmed lives are, without realising it, using basic principles to create good fortune.
    For instance, they seemed able to tell whether strangers were trustworthy within minutes of meeting them. To test this, the volunteers were sent a videotape of individuals telling the truth or lying and asked to pick out the liars.

"The lucky subjects were far more accurate," said Dr Wiseman.

The lucky and the unlucky also reported winning very different amounts of prizes in lotteries or raffles. But the research showed that the lucky simply bought more tickets or entered more contests.

"Those who thought themselves lucky thus increased their chances of winning," said Dr Wiseman. "The truth is that blind chance favours nobody, lucky or unlucky."

Psychological tests also revealed that the lucky tended to be optimists. "Their high expectations about future wealth, health and happiness often became self-fulfilling prophecies," said Dr Wiseman.

They were also quicker to exploit opportunities thrown up by chance. Their intuition, meanwhile, often proved highly accurate.

"They consistently display enough courage to make important life decisions on the basis of gut instinct," said Dr Wiseman

"Lucky people also persevere, do not use bad luck as an excuse for their own mistakes and always look on the bright side of life."

Dr Wiseman's research enabled him to produce a series of exercises that help people improve their luck by changing their outlook. Dr Wiseman said: "Once one understands the secrets of luck, it is possible to create a luckier life," he added

His findings are published in a book called The Luck Factor.

I can vouch unequivocally for the truth in his conclusions!

The reason that I've referred to it here is that it convincingly illustrates much of what I'm passing on to you.

M

MENTORS

I'm sure you'll find that almost every high achiever has benefited from at least one, if not several, mentors along the way.

Finding someone you admire, and possibly would like to emulate, is an important part of your successful career development strategy.

In most cases you will know them personally - perhaps even work for them. It is possible though that you may find your mentor through a book that you read.

Many people attribute much of their success to the inspiration and information they got from a motivational book, such as those written by Napoleon Hill, Tony Robbins, or W.Clement Stone.

Somebody I know very well, who has amassed a personal fortune in excess of 50 million pounds, confided in me that his most influential mentor was W.Clement Stone, *yet he never ever met him!*

I benefited a great deal in my early days as a young sales manager from reading a few self-help books, but I also benefited by the interest that two or three people took in my development and my career over the years, and I will always be grateful to them.

MONEY

It isn't everything. But it is quite high on the list! As I mentioned at the beginning of this book, for me (to use a Zig Ziglar quote) it's right up there with oxygen!

Frankly I feel that in our society it would be difficult to really enjoy life and be happy if continually having to worry about paying the bills – never being able to afford many of the good things in life. After all, life has so much to offer!

It's also my belief that you will eventually become as wealthy as you *decide* to become. Not what you would *like* to become.

Because accumulating wealth has a great deal to do with your attitude to money.

If you do the lottery in the vain hope that this will make you rich, you are making a clear statement that says, "I wish I was rich but I don't expect it to happen"

There's nothing wrong with a flutter on the lottery or the occasional horse race perhaps. But it should be done for fun, not as a strategy to become rich.

It's good to want to be wealthy but if you are depending on a chance in a million to determine your destiny, not only are you a fool, but you are also acknowledging to yourself that you can't see yourself becoming rich any other way.

If you've stayed with me up to this point though, I'm confident that by now you know better!

The trouble is that so many people want to be wealthy but do absolutely nothing constructive about it!

Money is good. For the good it can do. There's no sin in becoming wealthy. And there's no great virtue in poverty either.

But money is for using, not just for spending. *You are very unlikely to become wealthy on your taxed earnings alone, because we tend to live up to our income. The only way to accumulate money is to put money to work.*

Listen up. Here's the major lesson I ever learned about accumulating wealth.

Ten percent of all you earn is yours to keep – pay yourself first. That's the advice given in the book 'The Richest Man in Babylon'. It's great advice. Save a minimum of ten percent, invest it wisely, and one day you will find out just how fantastic that gem of wisdom really is.

When you get paid, and before deducting the income tax, your National Insurance contribution or the mortgage payment etc., work out what ten percent of your gross income is and tuck it away.

Every time you get paid.

And never raid the till! Keep your hands off it. Put it into a savings account each week or month (depending how you are paid) and as soon as you have around £500 invest it in a tax free ISA. Or better still open an ISA account that accepts monthly contributions. Remember this is a long term wealth strategy so you should have it in equity investments rather than cash. If you are new to the stock market you may decide to use a 'tracker fund' which tracks the FTSE 100 or the FTSE All share Index.

Over time these funds, which are spread over the largest 100 companies in the UK or all the companies listed on the main Index, have out-performed many of the specialist funds which are run by highly paid investment fund managers. The FTSE 100 over the last 40 years (1972-2012) has grown at over 11% a year. And that's not including the re-investment of dividends. Some years it has fallen but most years it has risen. But over the longer term stock markets have always gone up, and have risen faster than inflation.

There are a host of tracker funds which track other indices in addition to the FTSE 100 but if you are new to equity investment the FTSE 100 may be a good place to start.

Alternatively choose a fund that invests for high income and reinvests the dividends.

To illustrate the power of this it's worth quoting Neil Woodward, of Invesco Perpetual, who manages one of the most successful funds in the UK which has performed magnificently since its inception in 1988.

"Over the long term, the vast bulk of returns to investors come from dividends. Dividends are also the acid test of how much confidence a company has in it's own money-making ability because they represent a cash payment to shareholders"

I wish I had known this when I first started investing......it would have prevented me from chasing shares that I hoped would double in value overnight!

Let me share a bit more of Neil Woodward's wisdom.

"The discipline of buying only stocks that generate a solid dividend is a useful one because it tends to steer you away from frothy, speculative stocks. For example, during the dotcom boom I did not buy technology stocks because they were not paying decent dividends. I came under some pressure at the time for not doing so. but was vindicated when the tech bubble burst,"

Neil Woodward has made thousands of investors very wealthy over the years and is acknowledged as the leading UK investment manager over the last twenty-five years.

Now I know I have said this before: **Don't try getting out of debt first before you start doing this!**

Why do I say this so emphatically when nearly everybody else would tell you that getting out of debt has to be your number one priority? The answer is simple....I understand human nature.

How long have you had debts; outstanding balances on credit cards, or bank loans, or overdrafts, or maybe all three? Then what makes you think that anything will change? You'll soon give up trying to get out of debt unless your whole approach to money begins to change.

By starting to save, even though the interest or capital gains you will initially earn on savings will be less than interest you are being charged on your loan balances, you are embarking on a road that eventually will lead to wealth.

Soon you will be motivated to look at ways to increase your income.

You will become more prudent in how you spend. You will develop a much healthier attitude towards money.

Then you will be really eager to get rid of your debts. You will be motivated to take control of your spending. You'll look for ways to reduce your outgoings and increase your income. You will begin to willingly take positive actions to dramatically improve your finances.

As your savings and investments grow you will find yourself looking at new ways to invest and accumulate wealth. In my own case I primarily spread my investments between the stock market and property. That's not to say that there aren't other good forms of investment. Some people have made a lot of money by investing in art or fine wines for example. However these are specialist areas and you need to fully understand these markets before you go down that route.

Don't take undue risks. And do take qualified advice.

Whatever else you do, don't ever use this money to fund your lifestyle until you are able to retire. There have been many times in my life that I had a large overdraft at the bank in order to pay school fees and live the life I wanted to....but I never plundered my growing investments. *And I never stopped saving and investing at least ten percent of everything I earned.* There's nothing wrong in borrowing money from time to time, as long as your assets continue to far exceed your liabilities.

Most very wealthy people have acquired their fortunes by the use of OPM...other people's money.

This isn't a book on investment, but if you borrow money from a lending institution such as a bank or building society, at the lowest rate of interest you can get, and put it to work where it will return a higher rate of growth than the interest you are paying, then you will generate a profit or gain. Not exactly rocket science is it?

But don't confuse this type of borrowing with borrowing money to simply fund your lifestyle.

The best-known example of putting OPM to work is in house purchase.

Over the years it would have been difficult not to have made a handsome profit in the UK by buying a house and using a mortgage to finance a large percentage of the purchase price. Even though house values go down once in a while they always bounce back up again. It's a simple case of supply and demand.

Now, money on its own doesn't necessarily motivate, *but the lack of it always does!*

At first you may have difficulty accepting the accuracy of part of the above statement. However, think about it for a moment. The lack of money is a very powerful motivator – even to the point where people risk imprisonment for stealing or fraud. Most people are motivated to work to earn money, to seek better incomes and to get raises and to receive promotions etc.

Money is important, especially when you don't have very much. I know – I've been there.
But it's not really money that motivates – it's what money can do – what it can buy!
Money is a way of keeping score. A yardstick of success, an opportunity to compare ourselves to others. A means of plotting our progress.
It enables us to buy houses, and then bigger houses – cars, and then more expensive cars.
Money motivates because it enables people to enjoy a degree of recognition.

When you eventually have more than you can reasonably expect to be able to spend, the motivation will gradually diminish and other things will drive you to continue to achieve.

A few other thoughts about money…

Don't keep people, especially small tradesmen, waiting for it. Pay bills on time.
Don't waste it.
Get value for it.

Don't borrow from family, colleagues or friends. (Your parents may be willing to give you a helping hand, especially towards the deposit for your first house, but only accept help from them if you are certain they can afford it without incurring the need to reduce their own standard of living)

Don't make personal loans.

Protect your credit rating. It's vital. Under no circumstances get behind with mortgage or credit card repayments. Make sure you never have a County Court judgement made against you. If I'm too late with this advice you simply have to take steps to repair your rating and make absolutely certain never to let anything adverse occur ever again.

If you are uncertain as to what your rating currently is you should find out by going to www.checkmyfile.com and follow the instructions on this website.

The eighth wonder of the world – time and compound interest. (Rockefeller, Einstein or Benjamin Franklin? Nobody seems too clear as to who coined the phrase, but its truth is incontrovertible)

Much more on the subject of money to follow under **'Wealth'**

MOTIVATION

This is a scene from the days when my kids were much younger. (So was I, come to think of it!)

"James how many more times do I have to tell you? Get dressed!" This is my wife pleading in a raised voice with our young son for at least the fifth time in 10 minutes. He is not exactly the world's fastest dresser, since this is a regular routine on school day mornings.

I step out from the shower, towel myself dry and wander into his room. There he is sitting on the bed in just his underpants and with one sock on and the other in his hand as he turns the page of a book he is trying to read at the same time. My wife, who is trying to cope with our other little tearaway an eighteen-month-old human express train named David, called to me from the next bedroom. "Dave, please ask James to hurry up, he's dawdling away and we are going to be late." "James" I said standing in the doorway between his room and the landing, "I bet I can get dressed before you can!"

Instant action!

Less than two minutes later he comes dashing into where I am pulling on my trousers, now fully dressed, shirt, shorts, socks and jumper.

"I beat you!" he exclaimed in triumph. After conceding defeat and patting him on the back in congratulation, I nudged my wife and grinned. "See, it's easy when you know how!"

And it is.

People do what they want to do far more readily, eagerly and enthusiastically than what they have to do or are told to do.

All motivation comes from within. The only way you or I can affect others is by acting as the catalyst in developing the 'want to'.

Now that may sound easier than it really is.

For a start not everyone wants the same thing. And then not even to the same degree. And they may not want to make the sacrifice of time and effort required. Also bear in mind people will not be motivated to achieve or obtain goals that aren't consistent with their own self-image (take another look under the headings Imagination and Self-Image).

The skill in getting people to motivate themselves is to somehow help them develop a desire, and then show them how they can fulfil it. Keep in mind that only while the goal stays in sight will a person strive to achieve it.

Imagine taking somebody, who has never actually swum more than a few lengths of the swimming pool, out to sea on a boat. It's a fine calm summer day. Throw him or her overboard about half a mile from the shore *and he or she will almost certainly set an all time personal best as far as distance swimming is concerned!*

He or she will get back to the beach regardless. Even if it takes an hour or more!

Same scenario, but this time several miles further out on a cold and foggy day so no coastline is even remotely visible. The person thrown overboard would be most unlikely to survive for even fifteen minutes.

When the goal isn't in sight it is very tough to keep striving.

Now I'm writing this as if you are going to try to motivate somebody other than yourself. **But these principles apply to you.**

All motivation comes from within. And people who learn how to readily motivate themselves are far more able to ordain their own destiny.

So what is the secret?

Well, we already know that some of the strongest motivating factors are love, sex, greed and fear. Recognition ranks very high also.

These are strong emotions.

When setting goals you can be sure that at least one of these factors is involved.

This is the key. *Setting goals! And being dissatisfied with your current circumstances.*

Goals that excite you. Goals that will stretch you. Goals that will get you into action.

Write them down. Commit yourself to them. Think about them daily. Read them out loud.

And work to achieve them!

MAKING DECISIONS

Trivial decisions are no problem. Just follow your instincts.

But if a decision is likely to have far reaching consequences then obviously it can't be taken lightly. But agonising over a decision isn't really the best way either.

Each of us will do things differently but here's what I've learned to do, and I know others who take a similar approach.

First, gather all the information available to you and assemble the facts.

Make a list of advantages and disadvantages, if relevant to do so.

Think laterally and outside of the conventional.

Play the "what would happen if" game.

Consult, if you can, one or two confidants whose judgement you trust.

Where practical, sound out opinions.

Consider all the options available, and set a deadline for making the decision if one doesn't already exist.

Now, this is the fascinating bit.

Review all the facts, advice and alternatives and then commit the whole thing to your sub-conscious. In other words put it all to the 'back of your mind'. And, as the saying goes, 'sleep on it'

Where possible you should do this several days ahead of the deadline you've set.

In the meantime don't consciously think about the problem. Each time you find yourself thinking about it, push it immediately from your mind by thinking about something else. Force yourself to do this and just tell yourself that when the time comes you'll have the answer!

At the very moment you have told yourself you would decide, you'll find yourself clearly knowing what you plan to do.

The fact is that, although you stopped consciously contemplating or worrying about the issue, your sub-conscious mind will have been busy working on the problem the entire time.

So go with your decision.

Almost invariably it will be the right or best decision.

Often we will never know what would have happened had we decided otherwise anyway!

In nearly every case the 'right decision' turns out to be right because we make it work out.

And, in almost every instance, the only thing worse than a bad decision is indecision.

Remember what you read right at the beginning of this book. You are where you are today mainly as a result of all the choices and decisions you have made up till now and your decisions and actions will always be consistent with your self-image. So continue to work on improving your self-image.

MEMORY

How many times have you heard someone say 'I've got a terrible memory'! Possibly you've said it yourself.

If that's the case you don't have to ever say it again. Firstly, it's never good for your self-esteem to say or think negative things about yourself – and secondly it's simply not true!

Think about it for a moment.

Regardless of whatever age you are now, it's certain that you can recall hundreds and hundreds of events in your life. Schooldays, holidays, places you've visited, people you have met, parties you have been to, restaurants you've eaten in. The list of things you can easily recall will be fantastic. So much for anyone thinking they have a poor memory!

What most of us need to do is to develop a few good memory habits.

I'll cover one of these in more detail under the heading 'Organisation', but it's worth briefly mentioning here. That is to use a 'Things to do list'. Why make the effort to continually remember all the things you have got to do when writing them down is so much easier?

Another major challenge for most of us is remembering people's names.

How often have you been introduced to somebody only to realise to your horror two minutes later you've completely forgotten his or her name? It has certainly happened to me – loads of times. But not any more!

When I was a young sales manager I attended a meeting along with about thirty of my colleagues. The guest of honour that day was the newly appointed President of the Company who was visiting the U.K. None of us had ever met him before. We all briefly introduced ourselves at the start of the meeting. By the coffee break each of us was amazed that he could recall the name of every single person in the room. (We were not wearing name tags).

I have always remembered what a huge impression that made on everyone there, and I resolved to develop the same ability.

It wasn't very difficult.

The secret is to repeat the person's name out loud as soon as you have heard it.

So if somebody says 'I'd like to introduce you to Philip', reply by saying something like 'Pleased to meet you Philip'! Try to do this a couple more times in the next minute or so. If that isn't practical repeat the name yourself several times – 'his name is Philip... Philip ... Philip.

If you are meeting several people for the first time, for instance at a social gathering or a business meeting, keep repeating the names to yourself as you look around you. 'His name is John, her name is Sarah, his name is Mark, his name is Alan, her name is Kate' and so on.

If you're involved in conversation you can use the person's name. But don't overdo it of course.

People really appreciate somebody who takes the trouble to remember their name. They consider it a compliment – which of course it is. Try it – you will be amazed at how good your memory is!

Which bring us to another key to improving your use of memory.

Repetition

When you learned Poetry at school you weren't taught to memorise six or seven verses all in one go were you?
The way to learn something off by heart is to remember two or three or four lines at a time. Not fifty lines all in one go! By constantly repeating them little by little they stay fixed in your memory – and then you add the next bit by doing the same thing. How else would actors learn their scripts? ***Repetition is the key.***
You may hear a great motivational speech, but if asked a few days later to list all the key things the speaker said that had inspired you, you'd probably be hard pressed to remember more than three or four without looking at the notes you may have taken.

This is why I urge you to refer to this book many times, even if only for a few minutes a day. That's why it has been compiled for you to pick up time and again and open at any page.

N

NASTINESS

Is there any good reason to be nasty or spiteful to anyone?
Of course not! Being firm is fine. Nasty is not fine.
Be indignant by all means, if the occasion calls for it. And naturally you should stand up for yourself if being badly treated. But don't be nasty. It will get you nowhere.

It is appalling how some people treat others. Have you seen how some travellers give the airline check-in person a hard time when a flight is delayed? As if it was their fault!
Remember – what goes around comes around.

It's nice to be important – but it's more important to be nice!
There are many hotels that I stay in from time to time where I can always be sure of a superior room at no extra cost and a convenient

parking space for my car. Not because I know the hotel manager, but simply because I go out of my way to be polite and friendly to the staff.

NEGATIVE THINKING

It isn't difficult to spot negative people. They are the ones who walk around with a big black cloud hanging over their heads all the time. At least it seems that way.

They see the worst in people. They look for the downside in every situation. They are generally cynical and sceptical. They expect the worst to happen. They can brighten up a room simply by leaving it!

They give up easily – that's if they ever even try. They think they are unlucky.

And they don't think much of themselves.

They often blame everybody and everything for all their misfortunes, and never seek to accept the fact that they may be responsible.

Why can't they see the good in things? Even a broken clock is right twice a day!

If only they would change their attitude.

If you recognise any of these negative traits in yourself you must eliminate them. Smile more, laugh more, and look for the good. Act happy. Be happy.

And avoid mixing with negative people!

O

OBJECTIVES

It's hard to determine what difference if any, exists between objectives and goals. Perhaps objectives are more short term and goals are more long term.

But does it really matter?

Whether you refer to your aspirations and ambitions as goals or objectives is of little significance.

The important thing is to always have something to strive for.

OPINIONS

I realise that there's an enormous amount of things I don't know – but I seem to have an opinion on almost everything!

There's probably not too much wrong with that. I would like to think it's an indication of a high energy level and a reasonably active and enquiring mind.

There are some dangers nevertheless.

The biggest risk is closing one's mind and not listening to, or considering, other people's opinions. Also beware of the tendency to sound 'opinionated'.

Don't be bland and indifferent – ambivalence is not a leadership quality, but do be considerate of other people's opinions and be ready to let them express them.

In fact you will make friends and even learn a few things if you actually listen to other peoples' opinions!

OVER INDULGENCE

Can make you fat, or drunk. Neither is a pretty sight.

OPPORTUNITY

Go back just two or three generations to when your grandparents or great grandparents were young and you'll realise just what a fantastic world we live in today!

Seventy or eighty years ago most people never had anything remotely close to the choices and comforts that are available to us today. What a contrast there is between then and the way we live now!

Eighty years ago most people had not even travelled more than a few miles from where they were born. Those that had been overseas were probably sent there to fight for their country – and their lives.

Today the world is so accessible. Higher education is no longer only for the rich. Nor just the young.

We are surrounded by opportunities to improve ourselves, to make money, to expand our minds, to enhance our lives, and to contribute to society.

But if you don't have the right attitude, and if you don't have goals, you won't recognise opportunity if it came right up to you and stared you in the face!

You will only spot an opportunity if you are 'tuned in' and looking for it

So, whatever you do, don't let opportunities pass you by. Greet them, embrace them and take full advantage of them. Live life to the full!

ORGANISATION

Once in a while you will hear something or read something, which can profoundly change your life for the better. One such instance happened to me when I read a book by Frank Bettger 'How I raised myself from failure to success in selling'.

A great book with a great title. But it was Chapter Four 'Get Organised' that had such a positive effect on me.

At the time I was typical of so many young salespeople. Late with reports, shoddy administration, leaving all the boring jobs to the last minute, clueless about keeping track of my finances, no filing system, papers strewn everywhere and anywhere.

No doubt you get the picture.

I was an organisational disaster! Getting hold of, and reading that book could not have been more timely.

Here is the advice that Frank Bettger gave.

Set aside a specific time each and every week to take care of all the paperwork. Endeavour to do it on the same day and at the same time *every* week. Form the habit. Don't deviate, especially not for several months, until it has become a firm habit.

For me, taking care of household and personal things is something I now do for one or two hours early on a Sunday morning. If that's not going to be practical I will move it forward to Saturday morning. (Take note, I don't put it off to the following week!)

I made this part of my routine more than thirty years ago and it has never changed.

Take care of planning business things first (that's if it applies to you)

and then all the personal things like paying bills, reconciling bank accounts and credit card bills. Reply to letters. Write birthday or 'thank you' cards. Make sure your diary is up to date.

By doing this, you free your mind for the whole week ahead.

When bills and letters arrive throughout the week – just open them, and then put them in a drawer to be dealt with during your 'Organisation Time'!

Set up a filing system so you know where things are. Take some pride in being thorough.

I find that generally a couple of hours a week is ample. But you must do it every week. If you miss a couple of weeks, as is inevitable once in a while (if you have been on holiday for example), you will notice it takes so much more time to get sorted out and straight again.

I can't emphasise enough how much getting into this habit has meant to me. It's not a lot of effort. In fact it eventually saves you time and you feel so much better when you know you are on top of things.

The other important habit to get into is to use a 'Things to do list' and update it every single day. Simply write things you have to do on the list as they occur. Look at the list every morning. Cross things off when you've taken care of them. Rewrite the list every day or so.

The effect is tremendous. You will never forget anything. You will stop putting things off – at least most of the time, and you will get far more done.

If something seems to stay on the list day after day, as occasionally happens, then ask yourself why. Is it not really necessary? Or is it something you keep putting off because you know it will be either difficult or boring? Whatever the reason, you'll find you will eventually either delete it, as no longer necessary, or you'll force yourself to take care of it because you are so fed up with seeing it on the list!

You may find that carrying a few blank 3 x 5 cards in an inside jacket pocket to be very useful. It's not always practical to carry your 'Things to do' pad with you everywhere you go, so if you get an idea, or are asked to do something when you don't have access to your list, just jot it on to a 3 x 5 card and transfer it to your list later. Of course if you have an iPhone or iPad you can simply use 'Notes'

Finally, always put every forthcoming event in your diary. Never trust it to your memory.

At the end of the chapter in Bettger's book there was a great little poem. It was the last two lines that said it all.

> **'I'd do so much you'd be surprised.
> If I could just get organised!'**

OBSTACLES

Few things in life are easy. You are bound to encounter obstacles along the way. But if you are determined enough you'll find a way around them.

Just think about all those wheelchair athletes and blind skiers for example.

There are very few obstacles that can't be overcome. So let's see what *you* are made of!

P

PASSION

What a sensational word, even if a bit over used by marketing copywriters these days. But what a powerful force! Doesn't it perfectly summon up all the qualities needed to win?
Enthusiasm. Drive. Energy. Urgency. Focus. Determination.

And above all, a love of doing what you do!
Put all that together and nobody can stop you.

Whatever you do – do it with passion!

PAYING THE PRICE

If you want to be a high performance person you must be willing to pay the price. Sir Steve Redgrave didn't win five Olympic gold medals just messing about in a boat.

You can't have everything in this life. You have to be prepared to make sacrifices.

Winning those medals took hours and hours of training each day. Every day. For years. It meant rowing in all weathers. It meant intense pain and endurance. It meant a very limited social life. It meant foregoing many of the things he might have longed to do.

But that's what achieving goals and dreams is all about.

Those days, weeks and years of gruelling and agonising effort are all now in the past. Those gold medal performances will live on forever. Do you think Sir Steve Redgrave considers it all worth it? You can bet your life on it!

At the end of the day **you won't really pay the price of success** because it will all become worthwhile. **But you will pay the price of failure.**

What worse fate can there be than getting old and regretting all the things you didn't do?

Recently I was interviewing a very likeable young man, fairly new in his job, about his career aspirations. When I asked about his longer-term personal goals I found his response to be extremely profound.

He said, "I think the most important thing is that when I am old I don't want to have any major regrets".

For me that says it all. There is no such thing as a free lunch. You have to give up something to get something. But it will be worthwhile at the end of the day.

PRACTICE

There are no great performances without practice.

If you follow football you will recall a time when there were two players in the UK Premier League who were simply outstanding at scoring from 'dead ball' situations.

How did David Beckham and Gianfranco Zola become so brilliant at scoring goals from free kicks?

How did Cristiano Ronaldo perfect those fantastic 'stepover' skills?

Because they stayed on the training ground after everybody else had gone home and practised for hours!

Every great sportsman or sportswoman, every great musician, every great singer, they all practice, practice and practice.

If that is what it takes to become highly skilled at something then you know what you have to do don't you?

PROMISES

'A promise made is a debt unpaid!'

Don't ever make a promise unless you are sure you intend to keep it. Neither to yourself nor to anybody else.

People won't always remember the promises you have kept.... But break a promise just once and they will never forget!

Make them sparingly – and keep them all.

PERSISTENCE

Success is achieved by those who try and keep trying!

This is a slogan that decorated the wall of every sales meeting I ever attended as a salesman and sales manager.

In other words... Persistence pays off.

And it does. There are countless stories that you are surely familiar with, ranging from Thomas Edison inventing the light bulb to Robert Bruce watching his famous spider.

Persistence is powerful.

However, it doesn't mean that you should keep doing something in exactly the same way.

Remember the saying 'If you always do what you've always done, you will always get what you've always got'.

Persistence means keeping the goal in focus and continuing to strive to reach it, even though you may have to try many different strategies to get there.

Persistence pays off.

PREPARATION

Several years ago a piece of land adjacent to the office building where I worked was sold to a developer who built a large four-storey department store. From the day the work started I had a bird's eye view from the windows of my top floor office.

Digging out the foundations, and sinking huge metal pillars into the ground, seemed to take forever.

It really must have been at least nine or ten months from when the project commenced until anything rose above ground level.
Then three or four months later the roof went on and after only a further four months the store opened!

It took longer to prepare the foundations than it did to erect the building, fit it out, stock it and get ready for business!

'What does that tell me?' I asked myself.

Most of the important tasks that you or I may undertake will be performed so much better if the time is taken to prepare properly.

A presentation, a sales meeting, a written report, sitting an exam. Whatever the job, proper preparation plus proper execution equals success.

PROCRASTINATION

Procrastination is truly what separates failures from achievers. We've all heard the sayings: -

'Never put off until tomorrow what you can do today.'
'A stitch in time saves nine'. And so on.
Surely we must accept that these sayings, passed down through many generations, have enduring wisdom.
And yet putting things off still afflicts the majority!

Excuse me for mentioning it again but W. Clement Stone, who became worth many millions of dollars, attributed his success to these three simple words. **DO IT NOW!**

Most of the population are probably sitting on their backsides right now watching the television not even thinking about what they really could be doing.

So think how easy it is for you to stay ahead of the game if you just **DO IT NOW!**

POSTPONE THE PLEASURE

A major key to a successful life (however you define success for yourself) is the ability to 'postpone the pleasure'.

At its most fundamental, it's having the self-discipline not to eat all the sweets today so that you will have some to enjoy tomorrow. You possibly learned that as a child.

As you grew up you should have learned to put off watching television until you had finished your homework. Now you are an adult this discipline ought to manifest itself in the same way.

Don't spend all your money today – save some and invest it for the future.

If you don't have the discipline to save then you don't have the seed of success within you!

And you should continue to study and learn throughout your entire career in order to maximise your earning power.

This isn't to suggest you deny yourself forever, always postponing some pleasure.

That would be ridiculous.

The point is to enjoy today with all that it has to offer, but you must also master the art of postponing some of the gratification in order to enjoy even more of life's pleasures tomorrow.

Self-discipline, above all else, is what characterises the successes in this world.

The secret of happiness is enjoying today while planning a better tomorrow.

PROBLEMS

Somebody told me once that the only place you will find people without problems is in the graveyard!

Everybody has problems in their lives and in their businesses.

It's how you face up to the problem that counts. If you want to get ahead in business, the ability and willingness to help solve other people's problems is going to propel you forward.

Your boss doesn't want you to be forever bringing him or her problems – what he or she wants you to do is to provide solutions.

When you have to draw your boss's attention to a problem, as of course you will from time to time, try suggesting one or two alternative ways of resolving it.

There is very little that is insurmountable. Most problems can be overcome with some creative thinking, often through a team approach, coupled with a 'can do' attitude.

PERSONALITY

Personality seems set almost at birth. You only have to look at two young children in the same family to see how true that is. It's quite intriguing how different they can be.

Although it's fairly easy to modify behaviour – both our own behaviour and that of other people – it's much more difficult to change personality.

Seldom do people's personalities change dramatically. And when they do it is often through some dramatic or traumatic circumstance.

But each of us can improve our personality – if we wish to, and are prepared to work at it.

It's always a treat to be around somebody with a pleasing personality. Someone who smiles easily, someone who shows consideration, someone who makes you feel that he or she is pleased to see you.

Ask yourself how you think others would describe your personality.

Seeing ourselves as other people see us isn't easy, but it's essential to face up to facets of our personality which may irritate or offend.

Some people have a much greater need to be liked than others. But surely nobody really wants to be disliked?

And the more you work at liking others, the more you will find people liking you.

PERCEPTION

'Perception is reality'.

You're bound to have heard that expression. It has a lot of truth in it.
How you or I perceive a person, is what he or she actually is…..at least from our point of view. Naturally the reverse is also true.

Let's put this to the test.

Imagine that for a day you are a very wealthy and successful entrepreneur. You are wearing an expensive business suit. You look immaculate. You walk into Claridges with your Paul Smith overcoat on your arm whilst also carrying a beautiful Dunhill calf leather briefcase or, in the case of a lady, an expensive Mulberry handbag. You ask the concierge to look after your belongings and head straight to the restaurant where you have a reservation. You choose your meal carefully from the 'a la carte' menu and confidently order an excellent wine.

Needless to say from the moment you walk in, until you pay the bill, using a gold or platinum credit card, you will be treated with the utmost courtesy and respect.
And why not? To all intents you are a sophisticated and successful individual who readily commands respect.

Now let's 'fast forward' to the next time you go to Claridges.
On this occasion you are wearing the oldest clothes you can find. You haven't had a decent wash in days. Your hair is greasy. You look awful. Under your arm is a tatty dirty old sleeping bag. You plonk yourself on the pavement outside the hotel and start drinking from a beer can.
Do you think the hotel staff will treat you in the same way as before? Definitely not!

Here is the point. In reality neither of the roles you have played is the real you.

You know you were acting, both as a wealthy and confident businessperson, and also as a homeless 'down and out'.

In both cases you were not seen as the real you. Instead, you were perceived as the person you appeared to be!

Now I know this example is a bit extreme. So here's another one - a true one.

By some fortunate coincidence I read this the very next morning after writing what you've just read!

This is a direct extract of the autobiography of America's most famous and successful Chief Executive who headed up the world's largest company, GE, for over twenty years, Jack Welch.

"On April 1, 1981, I was like the dog who caught the bus. I finally had the job. Despite all the experiences that had gotten me this far, I wasn't nearly as sure of myself as I pretended to be. Outwardly, I had a pretty good dose of self-confidence, and those who knew me would have described me as self-assured, cocky, decisive, quick, and tough. Inwardly, I still had plenty of insecurities."

The message is clear

If you want to be successful - act as if you are already successful. Because you are!

Success is a journey, not a destination.

PRIDE

The saying is that 'pride goes before a fall', but I think that pride in this context could be better interpreted as arrogance or bigheadedness. There is nothing wrong with taking pride in the way you do things, pride in your job, and pride in yourself and your family.

Surely one day you would like to look back with a certain amount of pride in what you have achieved.

That doesn't mean that you have to lose humility or be immodest.

One day each of us will be aware we could have done better. But a certain amount of pride in what we did is going to be much more rewarding than being ashamed of what we didn't even try to do.

PLANNING

It's not often that a plan comes to fruition in the exact way that it was conceived.

It's an absolute fact that the majority of two or three year business plans rapidly become works of fiction. Regardless of how carefully they were put together.

There is always the unknown and unexpected that can never be totally catered for in advance.

But at least if you have a plan you know where you are starting from. And where you eventually want to be. Even if you only plan the first few steps.

It's no different from making a flight. During the journey the pilot or on board computer will constantly be altering the speed and direction and height in order to react to all the external forces acting upon the aircraft. Wind speed and direction. Weather conditions. Air traffic control instructions. The captain doesn't take off, point the nose in the right direction and then sit back till he gets there!

So what if you are blown off course from time to time? It's going to happen.

It's not a reason for not planning. Just permanently keep in mind where you are really heading and get yourself back on course.

Nobody plans to fail but the majority of people fail to plan.

POWER vs. CREDIT

If you manage people you must always give them the credit for their achievements.

Never try to take the credit yourself – even though you know you probably made a major contribution.

If you want to retain the power, give away the credit.

POSITIVE THINKING

I had never heard the expression 'Positive Attitude' until I joined an American Insurance Company back in the mid sixties.

The Chairman and Founder of the Company, W.Clement Stone, had co-authored 'Success through a Positive Mental Attitude' with Napoleon Hill, author of the most famous self help book of all time 'Think and Grow Rich'.

So it was hardly surprising that positive thinking was a strong culture running throughout the company.

Now, some 40 years later everybody has heard about positive thinking. You hear it all the time.

It's now become an accepted and global philosophy.

From which you might conclude there may be something in it.

Of course there is!

But what is positive thinking and how do you develop a positive attitude? Can it really make that much difference?

The answer is unequivocally – Yes it can, but you may have to work at it.

Whatever your age is, you will have established certain thought patterns and thought habits. This is as a result of many of the influences and experiences in your life so far.

Consequently some people find it more natural to think positively than others.

We recognise this positive tendency as optimism, enthusiasm, drive and so on. But, regardless of your natural tendency, it is possible to gradually and deliberately become more positive.

And here's how. (Yes I know that we covered this under the heading Attitude, but I make no apology for repeating the message. I can't impress upon you enough just how important this is!)

Positive thinkers characterise the 'plus qualities'.
For example: -

> Action as opposed to apathy.
> Honesty and integrity as opposed to dishonesty and deceitfulness
> Consideration as opposed to selfishness
> Kindness as opposed to spitefulness
> Generosity as opposed to meanness
> Courage as opposed to cowardice.

They exhibit self-discipline, and endeavour.
They look for the good in other people.
They look for the good in every situation.
They have a belief that 'with every adversity carries with it a seed of an equivalent or greater benefit' (my mother used to say 'every cloud has a silver lining!)
They look for reasons why something *can* be done rather than can't be done.
They are 'extra milers'.

Because they look for the good in others, positive people have learned to look for, and find, the good in themselves. And everyone potentially has some good in themselves.

So how do you develop these qualities?

By deciding you want to! That's how.

If you embrace most of the thoughts and techniques, and apply the philosophy shared with you in this book, you really will become a truly positive person.

You will attract all the good things that life has to offer.

PERSONAL TIME

Great as it is to be with friends, family and colleagues; everybody needs time to spend just with him or herself. Time to just 'be you', and to relax, reflect, think and unwind.

Make sure you regularly take time to find some personal space. Not necessarily every day but at least a few times each week, for an hour or so at a time.
  Don't count the time you spend driving as personal time.
  Indulge yourself.
  Read. Listen to music. Go for a walk or a run. Recharge your battery.
  It's good for you.

PERSUASION

The gentle art of persuasion!
Wouldn't life be fantastic if we could just persuade everybody to do what we wanted them to do?
Naturally that's not going to happen. But persuasion is a skill to be learned. And it's all about looking at things from the other person's point of view. What's in it for them? Each of us is much more likely to do something we want to do rather than something we ought to do. And we'd rather indulge ourselves than indulge others.

So if you want me to do something you should help me to *want* to do it. If you want me to believe something *show* me why, don't *tell* me why.

Right now I'm doing my best to persuade you to follow the advice written here, and to believe that it will all work for you, as it does for everybody who employs these techniques and lives by this philosophy.
By giving you this unconditional guarantee that your life can be fuller, richer and more rewarding, I'm hoping you will **say yes to success.**

PERSONAL SELF DEVELOPMENT

Strangely many people seem to believe the need for formal learning ceased when they left school or university. That's pretty tragic!
Life should be a continual voyage of learning and discovery.
And it's your responsibility. You owe it to yourself to develop and grow.

There's an overwhelming number of ways to do so. The only difficult issue is in knowing where to start!

Part time college courses... distance learning programmes... seminars... Open University Courses... conferences... reference books... clubs... associations, the list is endless!
There's no excuse not to expand your skills and to increase your knowledge.
You might want to *look* the same five years from now but surely you don't want to *be* the same!

Q
QUESTIONS

There is a well-known poem by Rudyard Kipling and the first verse goes like this: -

> **I keep six honest serving-men**
> **(They taught me all I knew);**
> **Their names are What and Why and When**
> **And How and Where and Who.**
> **I send them over land and sea,**
> **I send them east and west;**
> **But after they have worked for me,**
> **I give them all a rest.**

I like this poem because it is so simple, but contains such wise advice. ***This is the way to learn from people.***

Provided you don't appear to be interrogating them, people will respond willingly to your questions. Everybody enjoys talking about themselves - and most people seldom get the chance.

We can easily become so wrapped up in our own lives that often we neglect to ask others to tell us about theirs.

Show sincere interest in people and you will be astonished at what they'll tell you. And you'll learn so much.

Remember to use some open-ended questions that require more than a yes or no.

What? Why? When? How? Where? and Who? are such powerful words.

Using this technique is also a very effective way of encouraging people to open up to you as to how they really feel. Sometimes you will find that a person will totally and voluntarily change their point of view simply because you used this way of getting them to re-examine why they do certain things or believe certain things.

While we are on the subject this is a good time to ask what questions are you asking yourself on a regular basis? Questions that might start like….

How can I ………..?

What might happen if I did …….?

Why don't I try ………..?

Who might help me ……..?

When should I ask about ……….?

Where do I want to be…………?

You really should question yourself from time to time about how you are doing and how you might do more.

I'm going to be asking you some pretty important questions too before we've finished!

QUANTUM LEAP

Since life is so short and time races by, it's worth looking for ways by which you can take a quantum leap in both your business and your personal life.

How could you double your business next year? How could you multiply your wealth by three, four or more times over the next 3 years without putting everything at risk?

Although the answers won't come easy you'll never find the answers unless you ask the questions.

R

REPUTATION

It can take years to build a good reputation. But it can be destroyed in minutes! This is as true for companies as it is for individuals. Ask Gerald Ratner if you don't believe me!

One stupid act can undo years of effort. There are quite a few people who could testify to this fact. Don't ever risk becoming one of them.

REASONS

There are generally two reasons that people have for doing, or not doing things. The first reason, which they will readily tell you, is the one that sounds plausible. *Then there's the real reason.*

REPETITION

How many good films have you watched more than once? Probably dozens.

Isn't it amazing that, when watching a film for the second or third time, we see parts that we'd forgotten? Often films are every bit as enjoyable the second time around. It's the same with music. You are hardly likely to buy an album and only play it once!

Most learning comes through repetition. And I realise that I'm repeating something I have already said!

So I'm going to urge you to re-read this book several times. Get into the habit of dipping in for just 5 or 10 minutes every day. That way you will get the most from it and accelerate your success.

RELATIONSHIPS (Business)

There's a lot of truth in the saying 'it's not what you know it's who you know'.

It's impossible to put a value on having good relationships with people and building a large network or friends and acquaintances. You'll never know when you may need some advice or assistance. And you must always be ready to be of help to others.

Additionally it's much easier to meet somebody you may wish to talk to if you can ask to be introduced by a mutual acquaintance.

An enormous amount of business is done this way.

So, whenever you meet anybody, try to make a favourable impression. Show interest in them and be friendly. You have no idea when you might meet them again. Often in circumstances you may never have anticipated.

But build your network from the standpoint of giving rather than receiving. If people feel that you simply want to use them you will only succeed in alienating them.

Be genuinely open and honest and look for ways in which you may be of value to others. You must be totally prepared to do people favours with absolutely no expectation of receiving anything in return and with no ulterior motive or hidden agenda.

Over the years you will be paid back many times over. **And you'll lead a much richer and more interesting life.**

RELATIONSHIPS (Family and Friends)

For most of us the relationships we have with our family and friends is the most important thing in our lives. What would be the point of amassing a huge fortune and having nobody to share it with?

Whatever your background, and whatever your current circumstances are, you would doubtlessly acknowledge that maintaining and enjoying happy and harmonious relationships has to be constantly worked at. When you love and care for people you are bound to experience a whole range of emotions from joy to despair and everything in between. That's the stuff of which life is made.

Nevertheless if you are currently in a deeply unhappy relationship, especially if you are being mentally or physically abused, then you *must* break free immediately. The thought of doing so may be frightening but the consequences of remaining in such a destructive situation will be far worse. There will be help out there and you will regain your self respect. Hopefully you will eventually find a soul mate and enjoy a loving and caring future together.

Regardless of the pain, disappointments, hurt and worry you will inevitably encounter from time to time, there is surely nothing more worth striving for in this life than to love and be loved.

If you are part of a loving family and also have friends you care for, and who care for you too..... you are already rich!

Don't let the quest for financial wealth or career success take precedence over what really counts in this life.

READING

I'm referring to the activity rather than the football club!

There are probably more books in print today than at any time in history; and possibly with fewer people reading them.

But talk to any high achiever and I'm willing to bet you'll discover that they read regularly.

Whether fiction or non-fiction, it makes no difference. Reading books is not only a great source of pleasure and relaxation it's also a great mental stimulus. It's brilliant for the imagination.

Doubtless you would have noticed that I've referred to several books that have been of help to me over the years. Many of these were written a long time ago but could still be available from Amazon. However there are some excellent 'self-development' books that have been written far more recently and are easily available in good bookshops.

Don't become a 'self-help' junkie hoping that the next one you read is going to be the one that suddenly will make you rich overnight! That won't happen. However reading one or two a year should reinforce what you've already learned and keep you motivated, inspired and focused.

You can be certain of one thing though....*none of the advice or suggestions you read will work* - **unless you do!**

Books can be educational or inspirational or simply entertaining.

Don't deprive yourself – read some more books!

RESOURCEFULNESS

Nobody's going to sort out all your problems for you. Admittedly it makes sense to seek help or advice from time to time, but once in a while it's going to be all down to you. So you should learn to become resourceful.

Be creative and use some initiative.

Think clearly and, if necessary, think differently.

Look for alternative solutions that are not always the obvious.

RELIABILITY

If you are serious about success then be sure that you are totally reliable. Don't let people down. Demonstrate in every way that you are dependable. That doesn't mean being boring and predicable. It simply means that you keep your word.

RESPONSIBILITY

After all is said and done **what you do with your life is your responsibility**. Nobody else's.

You cannot abdicate from that. You can take the credit and must also take the blame!

So behave responsibly. Both towards yourself and towards others.

Look after your health. Maintain a sensible weight, eat properly, don't smoke, don't take any illegal drugs and don't drink too much.

Save at least ten percent of your income each month. Even if you currently have some debts.

Try to learn something new every day.

When at work show that you can take responsibility whenever the occasion or opportunity arises. Demonstrate that you have the ability to take control of situations.

Take charge and rise to the occasion.

RECOGNITION

We all enjoy it, even if we may be embarrassed to admit it.

There's nothing wrong in having a need to be recognised. It's what makes people strive to achieve. But don't become a 'recognition junkie'. That's a real turn off.

It's OK to have an ego. But don't let your ego have you.

Never compromise your standards in order to gain recognition. It would be a hollow victory.

People always thrive if given proper recognition for their achievements. Sadly some people work for years without ever having been thanked or recognised for their contributions.

Good leaders give proper recognition to others and constantly look for opportunities to do so. A pat on the back, a letter of thanks, a mention in a company newsletter – there are plenty of ways to make others feel good about themselves. You'll feel good for having made somebody's day.

RECORDS

People who keep records break records!

S

SELF-DISCIPLINE

We have already covered this under 'Discipline'.

I just wanted to remind you that self-discipline is the single most important factor that separates achievers from the rest of the pack.

SELF-ESTEEM

We all know how important it is to feel good about ourselves.
Building good self-esteem is vital and it is nearly always improved after taking some positive action.
Doing something you may be afraid to do. Achieving some 'wins'- however minor.

Overcoming inertia and doing something you've been putting off is good for improving your self esteem; and take into account that every time you let yourself down by not acting when you should you will feel your self-esteem drop a few degrees. Your morale will sink along with your self-esteem.
Action will raise your self-esteem much better than affirmations. Telling yourself you're terrific doesn't work for long. You'll know that you're just trying to kid yourself.

Acting 'as if', and looking the part and playing the part is much more effective than just 'thinking the part'. Because when you've done something you've never attempted before you feel good about yourself, even if you didn't do it that well.

Another certain way to boost your self-esteem is to make the most of your appearance. You know how good you feel about yourself when you 'look the business'.

In developing most of the skills you've already acquired, it's likely that your initial experience was probably a feeling of incompetence and embarrassment.

Riding a bicycle, skating, skiing, speaking a foreign language, driving, swimming, water-skiing, horse riding, speaking in public, all these activities, and many more, require some discomfort while learning.

But think how good you feel when you've acquired a new skill.

So get into action and feel good about yourself!

The more you do to boost your self-esteem the more your self-image will continue to improve.

SELF-IMAGE

How you see yourself is who and what you are.

But is your perception of yourself correct? Or are you selling yourself short?

This is at the very core of your being. *Learning this about myself and others was one of the most important discoveries I ever made.*

This statement – made in the surprisingly named but nevertheless brilliant book 'Psycho-cybernetics' by Dr. Maxwell Maltz says it all: -

All your actions, feelings, observations – even your abilities – are always consistent with your self-image.

It isn't easy to change your self-image. But you *can* do it.

Here are some specific things you should be constantly doing.

Setting and achieving goals – even if only small ones to start.
Building your self-esteem.
Associating with positive people.
Getting and staying in good physical shape.

Learning and improving new skills.
Using the positive power of your imagination.

These are all ways by which you will positively improve the way you see yourself.

STRESS

Much has been written and debated about stress over the last few years. So much so, that it seems as if a whole industry has recently emerged in 'stress management'.

There can be no doubt that our lives are much more stressful these days. We probably make more decisions in 24 hours than people living a hundred years ago made in a month.

Which route to take to work. What telephone calls to make first. What to eat for lunch. What music to listen to. What newspaper articles to read. What to wear today. What to watch on TV tonight. What to have for dinner. Where to go this weekend.

We are all faced with hundreds of options everyday.

Then there are deadlines to be met. Pressure to perform. Staying up to date with technology.
Relationships with family. Relationships with colleagues.
Constant communication through e-mails and mobile phones means there's virtually no 'hiding place'.
Yes, it's easy to argue that our lives are stressful.

But think of the positive aspects.

We live in exciting times. Never have we been more comfortable. Central heating, air-conditioning, comfortable cars, an overwhelming choice of food, supermarkets, shopping malls, leisure centres, holiday destinations.

Life certainly offers us a lot more than it did our predecessors.

Sir Michael Parkinson summed it up perfectly when asked several years ago how he coped with the stress of being a TV interviewer, a presenter and a journalist. He referred to his father who, when he was bringing up his family, had to get up at 5 am every morning, walk three miles to the coal mine, work all day down the pit, and walk three miles home again. For a pittance. 'Now, that's what I call stress', Parkinson said.

It's my belief that a certain amount of stress is good for us. It gets the adrenaline flowing. Most of us do our best work when under pressure with a deadline to meet; but keep in mind that it's also very important to keep your life in balance.

Take time to relax and unwind. Exercise regularly. Sleep well and get an absolute minimum of six hours a night. If possible take a catnap during the day. Fifteen minutes can really kick start you again. Avoid over-eating and drinking too much. Maintain your weight at a sensible and healthy level.

Stay positive and always have things planned that you are looking forward to.

SYSTEMS

Take a look at some of the world's best-known companies. You'll quickly discover that systems and processes, which can be easily learned and replicated, are the cornerstones of their success.

MacDonald's operate all over the world. The employees that work in and run their restaurants have an average age of twenty!

Many sales organisations owe their success to having developed a proven sales system that gets results time after time.

We all benefit from structure in our lives.

So work on developing a system that gets the most out of you.

That doesn't mean that you have to get into boring routine and never be flexible. But it does mean that getting into the habit of doing things in a certain way, or at a certain time, produces optimum results.

You will achieve much more.

T

TIME

In this world there is only one thing that everybody has in common. That's time!

Each of us has only 60 minutes in each hour, 24 hours in each day, and seven days in each week ... and so on.
    We can't buy it, borrow it, hoard it, or get more than our share of it.
    We can only spend it!

Just like money, what really counts is how you use it!

Time is what our lives consist of.

When, where, and how we spend our time is, in essence, what we are trading our lives for!
    Doesn't that thought make every minute seem important!
    None of us know how much time we have left in our personal 'time bank'. So whatever we spend it on should be of value and not simply wasted.

One thing is for sure, the older you become the quicker it will seem to go! A friend of mine proposes the theory that as each year goes by it represents a smaller percentage of your life so far!
    Whether there's any validity to that theory isn't really important. What *is* important is that we make the most of our time.

Putting things off... being disorganised... poor planning... staying in bed too long... loafing in front of the TV for hours on end ... being too painstaking over trivial tasks... leading an unhealthy lifestyle - these are the hallmarks of life's 'also rans'.
    Achievers do not succumb to those temptations. They know better. They have better things to do with their time rather than squander it.

    '*The difference between the rich and the poor is what they do in their spare time*' *(Robert Kiyosaki)*

I know it is a cliché, but we should try to live every day as if it may be our last; because one day it will be.

So live life to the full and make the most of it.

THINK

If I recall correctly it was IBM in the sixties and seventies that had signs hanging all over their office walls simply saying **THINK**.

Whether or not that had an influence on them becoming, at that time, one of the world's major 'blue chip' companies one can only speculate.

It would hardly be surprising however, if that singular word 'think' did have an impact.

Since most people really don't spend time to actually *think*.

Oh yes, we think we think. You could easily argue that unless we are thinking we must be asleep. I'll accept that, to a degree; but what is really happening most of the time is that we merely have hundreds of thoughts just running through our heads. Stimulated by what's happening around us. We aren't harnessing any real 'thought power'.

But all great entrepreneurs and achievers take time to really think.
They think about a current problem or an issue they may be facing. They think about opportunity. They think about achieving specific goals.

Learning to do the same, if you don't already do so, will make a significant difference to your life. But you have to take time to do so.

How to expressly do that will differ from person to person. You'll need to take regular time on your own. Set aside about 30 minutes a day. Be relaxed.

For me, some of my most productive thinking time is when I'm out walking or jogging. Other people might prefer to sit and relax in a comfortable chair. Or even in a bath.

There's nothing wrong in taking time to really think when doing something else; mowing the lawn for example. As long as what you are doing can be done on 'auto-pilot' and doesn't require any great degree of concentration

Recently I read of a very successful investment fund manager who claims to get some of his best ideas when he goes to watch West Ham play!

However you orchestrate it in your own life, get into the habit of taking regular thinking time and planning time. It will pay you back many times over!

TRUE RICHES

In case you are still thinking that this is all about making money – it's not.

Not that there's anything wrong in making a lot of money. There isn't. I've already shared my thoughts with you on that subject, and there's more to come.

Money makes most things so much easier.

But for most of us it takes many years to accumulate considerable wealth.

When I was in my twenties, buying a house and raising a family, I knew exactly what it was like to be broke.

I experienced the humiliation of having my phone cut off and the gas supply disconnected. I also still remember being away on summer holidays and anxiously wondering if I had enough money to last out the week!

Getting divorced in my early thirties and starting all over again didn't exactly help my financial situation a great deal either!

Now I have reached a point in my life when I can afford to do all the things I want to. Money isn't anywhere near the issue for me today that it was 30 years ago.

Why am I telling you this? The reason is simple.

You do not have to wait until you are financially secure and financially independent to get the most out of your life.

I've enjoyed every step of the way from when I was a hard up young salesman to where I am today.

And you should be sure to do the same.

For me, the true riches of life can be found and enjoyed in hundreds of different ways.

Here are a few things that to me have represented the true riches of life.

Seeing beautiful sunsets.
Waking up to a clear blue sky.
The memory of my kid's faces when they woke up to find Santa had been.
Feeding a baby at two o'clock in the morning when the rest of the world is asleep.
Watching my son playing football.
Watching his brother play cricket.
Walking down the aisle with my daughter on her wedding day.
Sharing meals with good friends.
Laughing at myself when I was learning to ski.
(Actually my family still laugh at me when I ski!)
Hearing the word Dad (and now – Grandad too!).
Marvelling at the fantastic shapes formed by a snowstorm.
Achieving something I have always wanted.
Walking in the countryside.
A glass (or two!) of good wine
Going to a football match with one, two, or all three of my sons (not easy these days as they live in three different countries!)
Attending our children's graduation ceremonies.
Beautiful music.
The colour of leaves in autumn.
Starting a long car journey early on a summer morning and watching night turn into day as the dawn breaks.
Eating outside on warm summer evening.
Watching my kids grow into nice people.
Family holidays and get togethers.
Working in the garden in the summer.
Not working in the garden in the winter!
Reading a good book.
Eager anticipation.
Making a sale.
Making up!
Waking up!
Thunderstorms.
Strolling along a beautiful beach.

These are just some of the things I have enjoyed over the years. There's a lot more to look forward to.

Your list may look somewhat different if you were to write it, but if you reflect for a moment as I hope you will, you will realise how truly blessed you already are. **Many wonderful experiences in life don't cost much money. They are the true riches of life.**

TEAMS

Several years ago my wife and I were in Ireland staying in a superb hotel, Dromoland Castle, which as the name suggests had originally been built as a castle. It was magnificent.

But being between Christmas and New Year it was almost deserted.

We were there because I was due to make a speech at a large sales conference the following day. Our hosts had graciously booked us in to this luxurious hotel because they were sure we would enjoy it. We certainly did.

During the afternoon I mentioned to my wife that I needed to prepare my notes for the presentation I was due to make. Rather than sit in the hotel bedroom we decided to go down to the comfortable drawing room and get cosy by the coal and log fire burning invitingly in the huge fireplace. We ordered some tea, which was ceremoniously served, and we sat back totally relaxed, thoroughly enjoying the tranquillity of our surroundings. I watched the coals glowing and the flames flickering around the logs thinking about what I would be saying the next day.

Suddenly one of the red hot coals fell out and settled in the grate in front of the fire. Within a few minutes it was no longer glowing.

And that's when it came to me.

You can't light a fire with one piece of coal!

Don't ask me to explain the physics – because I can't. But the fact remains. One piece of coal won't burn on its own. Take a piece of coal, that's red hot, away from the rest of the fire and it will soon stop burning! It's dependent on the heat from the rest of the fire!

That is how it is with great teams. Every member depends on the others.

Team members, properly inspired and led, will perform at a much higher level than ever they will on their own. Don't ask me why. It simply is that way!

No matter how good you are you can't do it alone.

You may be prepared to do the work of two or three people. It may be necessary to work that hard some of the time if you really want to achieve outstanding success. **But you can't *be* two or three people.**

Just as you may need to use 'other people's money' to assist you in building a business you also need other people too.
If you want to build a business you will have to build a team.

TRAINING

Peter Drucker, one of the worlds acknowledged experts on management, states in his best selling book 'The Practice of Management', "if you think training is expensive, just try doing without it!"

For most companies their biggest overhead is the salary bill. People cost money.
But people are also a company's greatest asset.
Read any annual report to shareholders and the Chairman's statement invariably finishes with something along the lines of 'Our greatest asset is our employees and we are indebted to them for their hard work and their magnificent contributions' etc.etc.
So make the investment in training. That's what the best-run companies do.

Now I realise that you may not have that authority right now. But if you do supervise other people, you can certainly take more responsibility for training and coaching them. Especially one to one; and perhaps as a group from time to time.
If you don't have anybody reporting to you then you may need to take responsibility for your own training programme.

Who can you learn from?
Who is qualified to help you do your job better?
There's always an answer if you look for it.

TRUTH

Truth will always be truth. There is no compromise. So don't ever tell lies.

I'm not suggesting that you shouldn't exercise tact and discretion in certain circumstances, but never deliberately try to mislead or deceive. Be honest in your dealings with everybody. It will save you lots of trouble down the line.

TALENT

Very nice to have. But it's not a substitute for hard work. And it's a crime to waste it.

If you're blessed with a special talent you will lose it unless you use it. So nurture it with practice and hard work. And be grateful.

U

UNIQUE

Walk down a busy street and look at the people coming towards you. Two genders, different heights, different weights, different skin colours, different hair colours. It's easy to see the obvious differences.

Now just look at the faces. Two eyes, two ears, one nose, one mouth.

It's hard to believe that with so much similarity no two people look exactly alike!

Even identical twins aren't totally the same. Their mother can tell them apart!

Not only do no two people look exactly alike, no two people think or feel exactly alike.

Every personality differs, possibly in some cases only slightly, but in many cases by a 'country mile'.

When you consider that there are over six billion people on this planet it's awesome to think that nobody is exactly like you. There never has been, and there never will be!

You are totally and absolutely unique!

So make the most of yourself.

V

VISION

Dreams come first. Yesterday's dreams are today's realities. Put another way, today's dreams are tomorrow's realities.

All great achievements begin with a dream. Dreams fire your imagination, they energise you into action. Without a vision you will never make real progress. You'll meander through life taking what comes.

If you have a clear vision of what you want, and where you are going, you will more easily deal with the challenges of today.

You will stay focused on the 'end game'. When you keep your attention focused on the goal a strange phenomenon occurs. You'll find yourself being transported into the future.

Eventually it won't be a case of *if* you get there; it will become a case of *how and when*. You'll start to assume success. You'll visualise it as if it were already reality.

Don't just talk about dreaming or visualising. Do it!

I can truthfully say that almost everything I have accomplished of any consequence I visualised and dreamed about before it happened.

If you focus really clearly on an outcome, you will find that when it happens it's almost like having déjà vu, the distinct feeling you have already been there.

When a 21 year old won the Augusta Masters in April 1997, with an unbelievable 18 under par, everyone was amazed.

But not Tiger Woods. His father told us that 'He's been talking about winning the Masters since he was five years old!'

Perhaps your goals aren't quite so lofty but whatever they are you must truly visualise yourself achieving them and know inside yourself that you will.

VALUE

Give it! Get it!

W

WEALTH

Although we went into some detail under the heading 'Money' there's more that needs to be added.

Not too long ago I held several career development training programmes for some of the more promising employees of a major International Company. One of the exercises I asked each individual to undertake was to write down anonymously what he or she would like to be worth in today's terms, (discounting future inflation) by the time they reached retirement age.

You would be amazed at the huge differences in their responses.

Their hopes and aspirations ranged from as low as £250,000 to as high as £10,000,000.

I'm sure that for most of the participants it was the first time they had ever even considered the question.

However realistic or otherwise their answers were, it plainly demonstrated that most people are prepared to go through life accepting whatever life dishes out rather than having any clear idea of where they want to be.

Now I have no idea what the concept of being wealthy actually means to you personally, and I can assure you that there is no right or wrong answer.

Anyway, as you go through life, it's quite possible that your aspirations could change.

Nevertheless I'm going to assume that you want to become considerably wealthier than you are today whatever the amount you have in mind may be.

If that's the case then there are several more thoughts and suggestions I'd like to share in addition to those under the heading 'Money'.

An important habit I got into as a result of the eventful meeting I had with my sales manager, back when I was deep in debt, was to take an annual 'net worth statement' on myself.

I've done it every year since for over 40 years, and you must start doing it too. I always do this at the start of every year. However you may prefer to do it at a different time in the calendar such as your birthday or the beginning of the new Financial Year. Whatever you decide, just make sure you do it at the same time every year. But if you've never ever done one you must do one now, today. If you've decided you are going to become wealthy you need to know exactly where you are right now.

I've always used a cashbook ledger for doing this but you will probably find it easier and more practical to use a spreadsheet such as Excel.

In the left hand column make a list all of your assets. For example:-

- The current value of your house if you own one.
- The current resale value of your car if you own one.
- The total amount you have in the bank or in savings accounts.
- The value of your investments in ISA's, unit trusts, company shares etc.
- The current surrender value of any endowment policies you may have.
- The realistic resale value of the total contents of your home and all your possessions (be very conservative here, as the resale value will be much lower than what the replacement cost would be).

There may well be other things to add, for example the current value of your pension fund or any investment properties you may own etc.
Make sure you list everything you own as if you were about to turn it all into cash.

Then in the opposite right hand column make a list of all your liabilities.

- Amount of Mortgage outstanding on your house.
- Mortgages outstanding on investment properties.

- Credit card balances.
- Personal loans outstanding.
- Bank overdraft.
- Unpaid income tax or potential capital gains tax liabilities.

Include any other liabilities you may have.

Then add up the two columns and deduct the total liabilities from your total assets.

Hopefully your assets exceed your liabilities and you have a positive net worth.

Don't despair if the number actually is in negative territory, even though it's not good news. Now is the time to resolve to change the situation as rapidly as you possibly can.

Naturally your aim from now on is to endeavour to see an increase in your net worth every year. But don't be too disappointed if once in a while you have a year when your net worth goes down compared to the previous year. This may simply reflect the market value of your assets at that particular time. We all know that share prices can go down as well up, and as we all know now, property prices can go down too, especially after a sustained period of rapidly rising values.

Get in the habit also of keeping a very good track of your income and expenditure. You should always know what your bank and credit card balances are. Check them at least every week. It's so easy to do now all this information is available on-line.

You may wish to use a software package to record all your transactions. Personally I don't use more than a fraction of the functionality available with the particular software I use (Home Accountz) but it provides the capability to produce records and reports in a number of ways in order to keep tabs on your money and investments. You can even easily compile an annual spending budget and keep track of it.

It's imperative that you live within your means. You have to ensure your income exceeds your outgoings and expenditure.

The more time you spend doing these things and consciously thinking about your income and expenditure, the more you will become financially astute.

Today there is so much that is available on the internet. If you feel you need a hand to start taking control of your financial situation may I suggest you go to www.moneyadviceservice.org.uk This will take you to a very well designed website set up by the government but which is funded by a levy on financial institutions. It is totally independent and unbiased. You will find it very easy to navigate around and use, and it could be instrumental in enabling and encouraging you to get to grips with your finances.

You really have to develop some financial awareness and then you'll begin to automatically take actions to attract wealth.

If you don't already read the money and financial sections of your newspaper then you must make the effort to do so. Every quality Sunday Newspaper has a good money section.

Not all their advice will necessarily apply of course, and occasionally I find myself challenging the recommendations in some of the articles. But it's only when you strive to understand investment strategies that you'll feel confident in taking more control of your money.

Be very cautious if taking financial advice from a Financial Advisor. Although today they are properly regulated, and they will have passed various exams to prove their competence to give financial advice, they are still likely to be out to sell you something even though they now have to charge fees as they can no longer receive commission.

I don't know of anybody who received advice from a Financial Advisor to invest in rare paintings, or fine wine, or property, or antiques, for example. Even though a lot of money has been made (and lost of course) by doing so. The reason is simple. If an advisor couldn't earn a commission or fee by recommending and selling something, then he or she would have been unlikely to do so. Furthermore another reason for exercising caution is that, believe it or not, many Financial Advisors are practically broke themselves, which does very little for their credibility!

I'm not trying to suggest you should never use the services of a qualified and authorised Financial Advisor, but do be careful of how you choose who to consult. My belief is you really won't need one until you have accumulated a significant amount of wealth. And by that time you will almost certainly know enough to be your own Financial Advisor! Better to get a good accountant, as your wealth starts to build, to ensure you don't pay more in taxes than you have to.

You can acquire a great deal of valuable knowledge by regularly visiting websites such as The Motley Fool (www.fool.co.uk) or International Investor (www.iii.co.uk) These are only two of several good sites. I've already mentioned that it's important to get into the habit of reading the Money and Business sections of your newspaper

I'm not authorised by the Financial Services Authority to give specific financial advice, but I can share with you some of my own thoughts and experiences for what they may be worth.

Firstly, I cannot promise that you will become rich in a hurry, although it is of course possible were you to come up with the right idea. Only recently I watched a programme on television (see, I do watch TV myself from time to time!) called Secret Millionaire. It featured a fairly young guy who had gone from nothing, to amassing a fortune of seventy-seven million pounds in only nine years!!!

We both know that there are plenty of so called 'get rich quick' schemes around today, as I've already said. Perhaps, with the prolific amount of internet marketing taking place today, there may be even more schemes on offer than ever.

I'm not going to say that none of these schemes work because I actually think there may be one or two that can. I have met one or two self-proclaimed wealthy individuals that assure me that they became rich through having attended a 'get rich' type seminar and followed the instructions they paid to receive. However, for every entrepreneur who claims to have made a lot of money from such a venture, there are thousands of people who have paid big money for courses, or attended expensive seminars, who have absolutely nothing to show for it.

One of the prime reasons for that of course is that they never did anything with the information they were given! That's because they are still only hoping to get rich as opposed to *deciding, expecting and intending* to get rich.

So if you do decide to fork out good money to subscribe to one of these schemes make sure you are under no illusions......they definitely won't work unless you do!!

Having said all that, I have to admit that personally, I didn't get rich quickly. To be truthful it took me many years of working and investing before my net worth first exceeded a million pounds. About thirty years in fact! But then I didn't know when I left school at 16 what I know now; and what you are hopefully learning here as a result.

However, only a few years after reaching that first milestone I became worth several times as much.

Go back and read the item under Interest (compound) and you'll understand how easily money multiplies once you have accumulated a substantial amount.

That's why it's so vital to start saving right this instant.

Money can't begin to go to work for you until you have some.

It's important to make clear that during the time my net worth was gradually increasing we were living very well. We found and bought the house of our dreams long before my net worth was in seven figures. We put our children through private school. We had at least two great holidays each year. We lived well.
So don't, whatever you do, deprive yourself from enjoying life now in the quest to build wealth. Because when you eventually become wealthy, you won't have a clue how to spend it! We've all read stories of sad elderly recluses who lived a hermit-like existence, and only after they passed away did it emerge that they were worth millions.
All you have to do is to take at least ten percent of your income (I say 'at least' because for every two years you are older than thirty you should add one percent; so if you are thirty-eight for example, you should be saving a minimum of fourteen percent and if you are 50 it should be at least 20 per cent) and invest it wisely. Spend the rest however you wish!
Money is to be enjoyed and life is for living

Let's talk a bit more about saving and investing ten percent or more of your income because, as you now know, this is the starting point of accumulating wealth.

You may be tempted to delay doing this until you are in a better financial situation than you currently are. If this is the case you are making a huge mistake and I guarantee you will be no better off in a few years' time than you are right now! You *have* to start now!
Putting it off is not an option.
Whatever your current circumstances may be, you just have to find a way.
What would happen if overnight the government added an additional ten percent to income tax? You'd have no alternative but to pay it, regardless of what you'd have to sacrifice as a result. So look at

all the things you are spending your money on and work out how you are going to manage on ten percent less.

I know that if I was to look at your credit card statements and your bank statements for the last six months, I would find there are lots of things you could do to reduce your expenditure. There are thousands of people and families living on a lot less than you are. So stop feeling sorry for yourself and just deal with it.

Now for the practicalities. Work out the exact amount that equates to ten percent of your gross income. Choose an equity fund that has a good investment track record that can be held in an ISA which takes monthly subscriptions, and then fill out the Direct Debit form for the appropriate amount.

Just as a reminder, the book 'Think and Grow Rich' is a great book, but its title may be misleading. You can't just *think* and grow rich...***you have to act also!***

If you were only to do this one thing you will eventually become wealthy beyond your wildest dreams. Even a hotel porter or car park attendant can become wealthy, especially by their own standards. Simply saving only five pounds a day, and never increasing it, would become close to a million pounds after 40 years if it grew at ten percent a year!

The average person is earning around £25,000 a year at the moment. I don't have any idea what your actual income is but let's assume it's around the average. If you become the person you are capable of becoming then I would expect you to substantially improve your income every year. It's quite probable that you will be making well over £60,000 a year within six or seven years from now if you have chosen to do so. Even if you don't aspire to a high earning career your income will still increase. So although you start out now by saving just £2,500 pounds this year, in a few years from now you could be putting anything up to £6,000 away. If you were to do the maths, using the compounding effect, you will see that you could reach a million pounds long before you are 30 years older than you are today.

Now there are a couple of things to consider. Thirty years may seem like a long time. But you are one day definitely (barring a tragedy) going to reach that point in your life. So do you want to be well off then or still be poor? The other thing to bear in mind is that the example I've given you is based very conservatively on you only saving and investing ten percent of your income at an average return of just ten per cent per year.

But in reality you will learn how to uncover many opportunities to accelerate the growth of your assets as you become much more financially savvy than you are right now.

However it's impossible to take advantage of investment opportunities if you have nothing to invest. You will also find it so much easier to borrow money for investing when you can demonstrate that you have already acquired a reasonable amount of wealth.

The one thing you will have to deal with is risk. In any investment there is always a degree of risk. Your attitude to risk is going to be an important factor and will be critical in determining your strategy. The younger you are the higher the risk you may be prepared to take. As you get closer to retirement you would be well advised to exercise more caution even though it might mean settling for lower returns.

Risk is a feature in all investment and business decisions and you should weigh up all the pros and cons carefully. Of one thing you can be certain. You will make some mistakes. Make sure you get it right more often than you get it wrong and always limit the downside. 'Don't ever bet the family farm' is advice I was given many years ago. In other words don't sign personal guarantees that could result in you losing everything you own.

Be brave but don't be stupid.

Get into the habit of reading the autobiographies of highly successful entrepreneurs. Amongst the ones I've read in the last year or so are:-

Duncan Bannatyne, who in addition to his autobiography 'Anyone can do it' has written two other excellent books on acquiring wealth and succeeding in business.

Peter Hargreaves (co founder of Hargreaves Lansdown) 'In for a Penny'

Richard Branson (we all know who he is!) 'Losing my Virginity'

Felix Denis (Magazine Publisher) 'How to get rich'

Peter Jones of 'Dragons Den' fame published Tycoon which is another book worth a read. Reading books like these will help you to start understanding the mind sets of rich and successful people.

When I think of all the wealthy people I know personally, I realise just how many ways there are to make money! It's just not that hard. But it starts with a *conscious decision, followed by deliberate and determined action.* And now you know exactly how to begin.

WHY – are you reading this?

Presumably in the hope and expectation that you will discover ways to put yourself on the 'fast track' to success. And you will.
    Provided you put into practice what you have been reading.
    It's no good just reading, nodding your head in agreement – and then doing nothing.
    None of this will work unless you do.

WHAT – do you say when you talk to yourself?

Of all the people you talk to, you talk to yourself most!
    Not out loud of course, but we talk to ourselves all the time.
    When you listen to that inner voice, what is it saying? Is it urging you on, or holding you back?
Be careful what you say to yourself – because you will believe it implicitly. And you will act and behave accordingly.

You know the saying: 'If you think you can or you think you can't, you'll be right.'
    Remember, you must be your own best friend – not your own worst enemy.
    So talk yourself up.

WHO – do you 'hang out' with?

The people you spend time with are definitely going to influence you. Make no mistake about that.
    So choose your friends wisely.

Mix with the kind of people you want to emulate. People who can have a really positive impact on your life.
    You need to be inspired – so seek out inspiring company.

Negative people will drag you down. Depressing people will eventually depress you.

If you need evidence of that just consider the fact that, amongst all the professions, the highest rate of alcoholism and suicide is amongst doctors!

It's a harsh fact of life that our environment has a huge impact on our emotions and thoughts.

Doctors spend so much of their time with unhappy patients, most of who are either chronically sick, terminally ill, or time wasting malingerers.

Not exactly the most positive environment in which to spend endless hours day after day!

Sadly, some doctors pay the price for doing so.

So don't voluntarily mix with groups who would drag you down – look for those who will give you a lift.

Beware also of people from the same background as yourself who may resent your success and try to talk you down.

The reason they do that is because you are making them aware of their own shortcomings and inadequacies and consequently you've become a source of discomfort.

Bringing you back down to their level makes them feel better about their own failures.

If you think these people are your friends then think again.

You need support, encouragement and inspiration from winners, not 'put-downs' from losers.

WHY – are you like you are?

A couple of years ago I was sitting in the back of a London Taxi travelling down Bird Cage Walk on a really hot and sunny July day....a rare occurrence!

Looking out of the cab window into St. James's Park I could see hundreds of people strolling or just sitting and laying in the sunshine.

One person stood out startlingly different from all the others.

Nearly all the men in the park were either in shirtsleeves without jackets, or dressed casually in shorts and T shirts, but this particular individual was wearing a long heavy black coat and waistcoat with matching black trousers. On his head he wore a large black hat. His hair was long and in ringlets.

He was of course wearing the traditional 'uniform' of his religion.

As London is such a cosmopolitan city it wasn't long before I spotted other people also wearing the various garments associated with their religion or culture.

Even though the hot weather might well have encouraged lighter and more comfortable dress.

As my taxi approached the City of London, where all the financial institutions are, I could see that there were fewer people dressed as tourists.

Here most of the men and women were wearing the usual dark grey or dark blue business suits.

What on earth is this all about? You may well be asking.

What I'm endeavouring to illustrate is that each of us, to a greater or lesser degree, are conformists. We dress mainly according to the 'group' that we feel we belong to.

If you aren't convinced then just look at the number of people, especially youngsters, who wear rings in their ears, eyebrows, lips, noses etc., or studs in their navels and even their tongues! Tattoos are currently commonplace.

There's nothing wrong with conformity. We all need to feel that we belong, and the way we dress and look is part of that process.

But so is the way we think.

And there lies the danger!

Each of us, since the day we were born, has been indoctrinated with beliefs, myths, standards, values, habits, responses and attitudes, as a result of all the influences our upbringing and environment has had upon us.

In the main that may be fine. But think for a moment. Have you ever really questioned some the things you were brought up to believe?

Especially about yourself.

Consider the extremism we unfortunately witnessed regularly during the problem times in Northern Ireland.

People born and raised in the same city, hurling missiles at one another. All because some were raised in a Catholic family whilst others were born into a Protestant family.

The tragic events of September 11th 2001 and the continuing conflicts in the Middle East serve to starkly illustrate the power of indoctrination and how insidious it can be when used to perpetrate misery.

Thankfully, people who are this extreme are very much in the minority, but it underlines how vulnerable we can all be, to the thoughts put in to our minds by other people. Especially while we are young.

The human species is tribal. Although superior to other animals we are still exceedingly herd like. As Maslow points out in his 'Hierarchy of needs' the need to belong is a powerful force. But it can be very dangerous to blindly 'follow the herd'.

What is it that you were brought up to believe that might be holding you back?

Isn't it time to maybe challenge some of the thinking you were exposed to when you were still quite young?

Here are a few examples of the things I heard repeatedly when I was a young man.

They went like this: -

'Why do you want to buy a house? A mortgage is like a millstone round your neck'.

'Cigarettes are good for the nerves'.

'Don't look forward to anything too much because you may be disappointed'.

'What's the sense of working hard, nobody's going to appreciate it'.

'There's no point in doing overtime because most of what you earn goes in tax'.

'The only way I'll ever be rich is if I win the pools'

Many of these misguided statements, and other similar examples of low expectation, were typical of the talk I heard in the bars of the pubs I frequented in my late teens and early twenties.

Thankfully I never allowed this kind of negative thinking to deflect me from my personal goals. Sadly many people did. That's if they had any goals in the first place!

We are all products of our environment and all the influences brought to bear on us over the years.

Nevertheless we don't have to be hostage to them.

Now is a good time to reflect on where you came from.

Cherish and hold on to all the positive and wholesome things you were taught, and reject and discard all those myths that may be detrimental or harmful to your happiness and your future success.

WHEN – will you get into action and live up to your potential?

WILLPOWER

The same as self discipline of course.

Don't tell me, or tell yourself for that matter, that you haven't got any. That would be pathetic. You didn't stand in line to have it doled out when you were born, only to discover they had ran out of it when you got to the front of the queue! You develop willpower in the same way as you develop muscle. Through exercising it.

So get tough with yourself. No excuses!

WRITE

The power of a letter can be awesome. I have endeavoured to teach this whenever I have been conducting a management development programme.

I'm not talking about emails and I'm not talking about memos. Even though, to a lesser degree, they can be fairly effective and sometime emotive.

What I'm really talking about is a real letter to somebody.

Preferably in your own handwriting. Nevertheless, a typed letter is also OK, especially when copying in other people. But always be sure to sign it personally.

So what kind of letter am I talking about?

Try a letter of thanks or a letter of congratulation. Even a letter acknowledging effort or progress.

You simply cannot put a value on it when written sincerely and

genuinely.

No recipient of that kind of letter ever throws it away! Why? **Because they'll read it over and over again.**

And they aren't accustomed to getting letters or hand written cards like that!

Another time when a letter can be really effective is when you have a need to express how you feel. Particularly to someone really close to you; a partner or a son or daughter

There have been a few occasions in my life when it's been easier to communicate my feelings in writing rather than by talking face to face. No need to go into detail. I expect you've had situations in your own life of a similar kind.

Never underestimate the effect a letter will have. This should be a warning never to write what you might regret. You can't ever take it back.

Try writing a letter to somebody saying how you much appreciate or admire what he or she has done. You'll never need persuading again. The impact you'll make will speak for itself!

X

X – FACTOR

An old pal of mine often used to refer to the 'X-factor'. You never know when it will show up and 'throw a spanner in the works'.

It doesn't matter how well you may plan something, or how cleverly thought out your strategy may be. Just when everything seems to be going great – up comes the very thing you would never have expected.

The X-factor!

Not always of course. But once in a while something will occur to scupper your brilliant scheme, which you could not possibly have foreseen.

It happens to everyone so don't feel too sorry for yourself when it

happens to you.
Take it on the chin pick yourself up and decide to get over it.

Look for the 'seed of an equivalent or greater benefit' and then move on.

Y

YOU

You are the most important living person – *as far as you are concerned.*

Of course I hope there are other important people in your life, but the only person you are with constantly, twenty-four hours a day, every day – is yourself.

So you really ought get to like yourself! And become you own best friend.

Just as you would wish for your best friend, you too must want to live a happy and fulfilling life.
All of what you have been reading comprises my sincere and best attempt to assist you in doing so.

Remember – what you are encountering in this book is the wisdom and best practice distilled from scores of successful people that I've met, plus my own personal experiences, and the many outstanding books that I have read over the years.
What I have *not* endeavoured to do is to guide you into being some sort of 'clone'.
You are you. There is nobody else exactly like you; you must be true to yourself.

But try to be a 'better self', through the way you think and the way you behave. There's no need to relinquish your individuality. Just work on becoming a more successful individual!

Look at the society we live in. Less than one percent of the population in the UK are super rich with wealth of several millions, or even billions, of pounds. (Not all of them are happy – but I can't for the life of me think why! Probably they neglected to keep their life in balance.)

In all honesty, I can't promise you that by following all the advice and philosophy in these articles you will definitely join this group. But you never can tell!

But here's what you can and should aim for, especially if financial independence is on your list of what you want to achieve: -

About five percent of people achieve a considerable degree of financial independence by the time they are in their late 40's or early fifties.

- They live in fairly comfortable and desirable houses in the upper end of the market. With either no mortgage or only a very small one.
- They drive prestige cars, which they can afford to change every 3 or 4 years.
- They take at least one, and often two or three holidays a year.
- They have enough money for anything they need.
- They have savings and investments and have secured an ongoing income for their retirement, which will enable them to continue their lifestyle after they stop working.
- They can afford good clothes, eat out in good restaurants, and above all have the freedom to pretty much buy whatever they really want.

They may not be exceedingly wealthy, but they certainly enjoy an enviable lifestyle.

This is not a bad target to aim at!

Consider the alternatives: -

About sixty-five percent are scraping along week-to-week, month-to-month. Just about keeping their heads above water. If they have any equity at all it will be in their houses. But they are mortgaged up to the hilt. They have hardly any savings and generally have very little money left over to indulge in any luxuries. A big unexpected bill could represent a major problem.

In other words money is a constant issue – or rather the lack of it is.

The remaining twenty-nine percent of the population are living a nightmare existence with crippling debts and no obvious way out. In most cases they are paying the price of years of laziness, disorganisation, a complete lack of self-discipline and sheer stupidity.

It's not a difficult choice to know which group you would prefer to eventually belong to is it?

Where you end up is up to you. You are the master of your fate and captain of your own destiny.

Your future is not a matter of chance. It's a matter of choice – your choice.

But there is a price to pay. Remember you can't have everything. Every decision you take has its consequences.

> If you want to lose weight you can't go on eating too much. If you want to get fit you have got to work up a sweat through some hard and regular exercise.
> If you study you will have to cut down on doing other things.
> If you have decided to become a doctor you can't train at the same time to become a commercial airline pilot.
> If a woman wants to raise a family she may have to put her career on hold – at least temporarily.
> If you want to save some of your income, you can't spend it all now.
> If you buy an old house to do up yourself, you won't to have much time for the cinema or golf. Your social life must take a back seat.

There's nothing for nothing in this world.
Big dreams come with a hefty price tag.

Only you can decide what is right for you – and what price you are prepared to pay.

But is failure really an option? I don't think so.
One of my favourite speakers - the late and much missed Zig Ziglar - summed it up perfectly by saying *'you don't pay the price of success – you enjoy the price. You only pay the price of failure'*.

So here we are then. **It's time for you to choose.**

Will you put this book away never to be looked at again – or will you incorporate the philosophy of success into your own life – and visit these pages regularly to keep you focused, motivated and moving in the right direction?

The choice is yours. It's up to you!

Z

ZEST

Put some in your life.

ZZZZZZZ

Sweet dreams. May your dreams become reality!

How high will *you* fly?

"It's your attitude, not your aptitude, that will determine your altitude in life" – Zig Ziglar

Back at the end of the 60's, when I first attended training school in order to become an insurance salesman, we were given a set of sales manuals. There were five of them.

When I had completed the training, and after several miserable weeks of selling very few policies, I became convinced that there must be a sixth manual that nobody had given me.

What was it the successful salespeople knew that I didn't?

Soon I was certain that I'd missed out on something during our training course.

It didn't occur to me that the successful people were simply putting into practice what they had been taught.

This was a lesson that it took me some time to learn.

A few years later, when I had become a regional manager, I learned another very valuable lesson.

At that time in the United Kingdom, not many people would have heard expressions such as goal setting and positive thinking, but working for an American company we were exposed to these concepts regularly

Quite often a shipment of a recently published 'self-help' books would arrive from our Head Office in Chicago.

Over a period of two or three years we received several different books which we distributed to our sales force with the suggestion that they read them. Many of them did, and a few obviously benefited, as was evident from their improved results and attitudes.

Nevertheless it was equally evident that reading these books had absolutely no effect on the majority of the people who read them. It took me quite a long time to establish just why this was so.

Knowing what I do now, I realised that their self-image was the major factor. These people just simply couldn't see themselves becoming successful. *All their lives they had been programmed for mediocrity.*

What was actually happening was that the people who were putting into practice what they had been reading began to get better results.

As their results improved so did their self-esteem, which positively impacted their self-image.

But what became abundantly clear is that many people ridiculously believe that just reading a self-help book is going to act like a magic wand - and suddenly their life is going to be transformed. ***That's as stupid as believing you only have to join a gym to lose weight!***

If you think that just by having read this book your life is going to instantly and dramatically change for the better then you are living in cloud cuckoo land!
Unless you act nothing will happen.

Only if you get into action will you gradually start to raise your expectations of what you are capable of achieving.

There was no sixth manual.

It's long been my contention that we don't incorporate nearly enough success principles in our education systems in schools. But you can no longer use that as an excuse.

Everything you need to know about becoming successful you have read in this book. It may not be a literary work of art - I would be the first to admit that I'm no great shakes as an author - but I have gone to considerable lengths to leave nothing out.

But perhaps a great deal of what has been documented here you already knew!
You just haven't regularly been putting it into practice.

So you now have the knowledge. **But knowledge is only power if you use it.**

To kid yourself that you need to read another self-help book, or listen to another motivational speech or attend a 'happy clappy' seminar before you get started on your journey to success, is just an excuse for doing nothing and staying as you are.
What you actually need to do is to get started. Now!

That doesn't mean you should never read another motivational book or listen to a motivational talk. Of course you should. They will help keep you focused and will help re-inforce what you've been reading here.

But before you read another book I strongly urge you to read this one again. Re-read it from start to finish and, when you have done so, get in the habit of opening it up at any page and reading for just five or ten minutes at the most every day.
Be assured that if you read it several times, it won't make *me* any richer. You'll only pay for the book once however many times you read it, but I guarantee that it will make *you* richer and more successful. Which presumably is why you bought it in the first place.

Don't start looking for the magic ingredient of success elsewhere. There is no magic ingredient to be found anywhere. **You are the magic ingredient.**

You will perform magic if you will just follow this **Formula for Success.**

The Success System

So here it is. Everything we've covered condensed into one easy seven part formula:

- **Develop and maintain a POSITIVE ATTITUDE**

- **Sustain a high level of PERSONAL AMBITION (Goals)**

- **Acquire the necessary know-how and PRACTICAL ABILITY**

- **Engage in PURPOSEFUL ACTIVITY**

- **Build in PERIODIC ACCOUNTABILITY**

- **Practise SELF DISCIPLINE**

- **Maintain your ENTHUSIASM and PASSION**

Of everything you've read, if you remember nothing else, make sure that you incorporate this 'formula for success' into your life from now on and forever.

From now on it's up to you.

If you've done what I've tried very hard to persuade you to do, you will have by now written down some exciting and challenging goals.
  Take them and read them.
  Make sure that they are still relevant. Do they need any modifying? If so, now's the time to make any changes.
  Are you serious about achieving them?

Provided the answer is 'Yes' then you must now take the first step.

Remember, you don't need all the answers as to how you are going to get where you want to be. You only need to know the first few steps. As you move forward, the way to achieving all that you want will become clearer. Just stay focused.

Before leaving you to achieve your dreams there are two more things I want to do.
  I'm going to give you a powerful technique, which will enable you to easily overcome inertia and maintain your momentum.
  Then I'm going to share with you a truly inspiring experience.

First the technique: -

This is something that I learned for all the wrong reasons!

Back in the late Sixties the founder of the company I was working for visited the UK to meet with the UK sales force at one of our quarterly sales conferences.
  Before finishing his speech he threw out a challenge to everybody in the audience.
  He asked each of us to design a simple chart listing seven important activities that we should engage in on a regular basis. We were then asked to make a grid listing the seven activities down the left hand side,

and put the five working days of the week along the top.

He told us to do thirteen of these, all identical, so that they covered a complete quarter.

Here was the challenge. We were to complete the grid every day indicating whether or not we had performed each activity. A simple tick would suffice to show that we had.

Our instructions were to submit the completed form at the end of each week to our Head Office in London. At the end of the quarter everybody who had completed and submitted all thirteen forms, regardless of how many ticks they contained, would receive a cheque for £500!

Here's the amazing thing. I think I was the only one to follow those instructions for thirteen straight weeks and get paid!

I really needed the money!

Now, as I've already told you, I did this for all the wrong reasons. At the time I wasn't in the least bit interested in developing better work habits; it was simply a way to make some much-needed cash.

Five hundred pounds in 1967 was a huge amount of money. At least it was to me!

By now I expect you know what's coming. You're right. That quarter was the best I'd ever had up to that time as far as my sales results were concerned!

Fortunately I recognised the power of this technique and subsequently used it and also taught it to many others during my career.

Since I have no idea what is going to be important to you, as far as activities are concerned, you are going to have to develop your own grid if you use this idea.

Make sure though, that you focus only on key activities that are critical to producing results. They don't have to be activities that you must engage in daily. Some may only be necessary once or twice a week.

For instance, in my own case, I would only hold a Sales Meeting once a week.

As an illustration, I have drawn one here as an example of what it could look like, based on the one I used as a sales manager.

Weekly Activity Analysis

	Monday	Tuesday	Wednesday	Thursday	Friday
Make 10 Sales Calls	✓	✓	✓	✓	
Field Train Agent	✓		✓		
Conduct Interview		✓			✓
Hold Sales Meeting	✓				
Recruiting Activity				✓	✓
Analyse Results	✓				
Prepare for Meeting					✓

Over the years I've seen and heard several other versions of this technique.

Norman Levine, one of America's most successful and well-known sales executives, attributed this simple strategy to his phenomenal success in training and developing high flying sales agents. He taught them to use a points system. It works like this: -

Making a telephone call to a prospect	1 point
Holding a meaningful conversation with the prospect	2 points
Making an appointment	3 points
Keeping an appointment	4 points
Making a sale	5 points
Getting a referral	4 points

Every day each sales agent has to aim at achieving 40 or more points. These can come from any combination of the above. Any shortfall has to be made up, so that at least 200 points are clocked up by the end of the week.

This simple yet incredibly effective tool for monitoring activity was, according to Norman Levine, one of the most important factors in enabling him to consistently be his company's top sales manager year after year.

Frankly I think this points system is the better of the two. It's easy to set up so you can keep score on yourself and analyse your activities, especially if you use an Excel spreadsheet on a Personal Computer.

I've lost count of the number people who have told me how much they have benefited from adopting this method

To be honest, I had stopped doing this myself since I ceased to work as a full time company executive, and was only reminded of it again quite recently.

So by now you must have got the idea.

If you want to sustain your activity level, and force yourself into developing good work habits, this particular technique is just fantastic!

Make a short list of what important activities you should engage in on a regular basis. No more than six or seven. Decide upon your own method of keeping score, and do it every day.

By devising your own system you'll take ownership and be absolutely amazed at how brilliant it is.

Now for the story: -

A few years ago I drove about 40 miles from my home to the small village of Selbourne in Hampshire. My mission was to buy some paintings.

There are several art galleries in and around Henley-on-Thames where I live, so you may well be wondering why did I go to Selbourne?

Well it happens that in Selbourne is the only shop of its kind in the country.

At the time, a man named Tom Youndle was running it.

I'm not sure if he still manages the shop now, but if not it will certainly be managed by one of his contemporaries.

Tom was an inspiration to me that day.

He showed me painting after painting, a few of which he had painted himself. He took them off shelves and out of cupboards. He put them against walls so I could get a good look at them. He put those that I rejected back from where he had taken them.

After I had eventually chosen to buy two of them he carefully wrapped each one separately and put them both in a bag.

He then took my credit card, completed the transaction, and wrote out a receipt.

What's so inspiring about that you may well ask? I'll tell you.

Tom has no arms!

He was born a victim of the thalidomide drug. Where you and I have arms Tom has just tiny flippers.

He does almost everything that you and I do with our hands, by using his feet.

Tom is a member of a group of people known as the Mouth and Foot Painting Artists. They paint by holding a paintbrush either in their mouth or between their toes.

It's quite probable that you have seen their work in the form of greeting cards or calendars.

They operate as a co-operative and market their work on a commercial basis. The shop is where you can buy the originals. They are not looking for charity.

Some of these artists were born with their disability and the others were disabled as a result of either accident or illness. None of them are able to use their hands.

Yet every one of them can paint beautiful pictures!

Now we can assume that, in all probability, had each of them been born fully able- bodied, or had not lost the use of their arms and hands, they might never have picked up a paintbrush in their life.

They may never have discovered and nurtured the talent that was residing within them!

We can be certain that none of them would have developed anything near the ability to use either their mouth or their feet almost as effectively as we use our hands!

Only necessity encouraged and required them to do that.

So what does this mean to you?

I'll tell you what it means to me.

It tells me that, without exception, we all have talents and abilities just waiting for us to discover and use.

There is potential greatness within everyone.

It would be a tragedy if you went through your life with your music unplayed.

Are you ready to live up to your potential?

It is my sincere wish that, in some way, what I have endeavoured to share will encourage you to discover just how high you can fly.

A special message if you are still in your twenties

I was twenty-two when I got one of the best bits of advice I've ever received. It was from a lovely old Scotsman, Albert Turtle, who was my boss when I worked in a department store. The advice was simple. And it got me into a habit that has had such an amazing effect on my life. Especially as my life is today.....some fifty years later. He told me to take out a savings plan. And I did.

Until then I always spent whatever I was earning. That advice changed my life, and I'll always be grateful that Albert persuaded me to save some of my income on a regular basis, even though there were lots of things I still wanted to spend my money on.

Lots of other good advice came my way in the years that followed. I think people in their twenties are very open to advice and suggestion. People are much more impressionable when they are young. They want to learn and improve themselves. And they want to emulate those that they hold in high regard.
    I know that I did, and I really hope that you do too.

So please think of this book as being especially for you.

I was lucky because much of what I've shared here I learned early in my career. Many readers of my original book have told me they wish they'd known all this while they were still young.
    Many have wondered why they weren't taught these things in school.

It's never too late to make positive changes in your life, but with every passing year it can become more difficult.
    Habits of both thought and behaviour become more and more ingrained and difficult to change as we get older. It takes a lot of resolve and determination.

The consequence of what we do or don't do today, may only manifest itself many years later.
That's where you have a real advantage. Time is on your side....because you're young.

Nobody becomes wealthy overnight. It takes time.

Nobody is going to die from smoking one cigarette. It takes time.

Obese people didn't get that way overnight, and they won't get slim overnight either. It takes time.

Nobody will start a new job today and get promoted to the board of directors tomorrow. It takes time.

You have time so don't waste it.

Because time flies.

It's very hard to think long term when you are at the threshold of your adult life. There are so many pleasurable distractions and exciting challenges that confront you. It's easier to live for today and hope that tomorrow will take care of itself. That's what most people do. And become full of regret it when it's too late. Clocks don't run backwards.

Of course I'm aware that the world we live in today is very different from the one in which I was raised. You may well ask how would I know what it's like to be a young adult today compared to forty-five or fifty years ago. That's a fair question. However although I don't propose to know specifically how today's environment impacts you, compared to life back in the sixties, I have a feeling that not that much has really changed.

Technology has made a massive difference to how we may conduct much of what we do today, especially in terms of communication, travel and entertainment etc. and life is undoubtably better for it.

But I bet most young adults still experience the same emotions, hopes, fears, anxieties, challenges and aspirations as I and my generation did at your age.

That's why I want to leave you with these few thoughts and suggestions.

Enjoy whatever you do.

In all probability you are going to spend 45 years working. The most important thing is to enjoy what you do.

You may already know what you want to do for a living. Maybe become a doctor, a lawyer, an engineer, or a teacher perhaps? Instead you might want to go into business. Whether professional or vocational it really doesn't matter. But make sure it's something that you find fulfilling.

You'll easily know if you enjoy what you do because you won't spend time wishing you were doing something else.

Personally I never had a clear idea of what I wanted to do when I was young. I eventually chose selling as it seemed to offer rewards based on results and ability. I've no regrets but I envied those who seemed to know from an early age exactly what it was that they wanted to do.

If you already have a career plan then I congratulate you and wish you every success.

But don't be concerned if you have yet to decide. Just make sure you enjoy what you do in the meantime.

Life isn't all about seeing how much money you can make. It's far more about being happy. Money is only really important when you don't have enough to enjoy a decent standard of living. I'm sure that will never be a problem for you.

Don't stop learning.

Just because your formal education may have finished when you left school or graduated from University your education hasn't finished.

In addition to learning the skills and knowledge required to perform whatever is essential to your job, you must continue to learn.

A new language, how to cook, how to fly a plane, how to ski, how to scuba dive... just a few of the thousands of things you can learn to do. And one thing you really must acquire is financial knowledge.

Your life will be so much more rewarding if you constantly seek to improve yourself.

You will also become a much more engaging person by regularly adding to your store of knowledge and skills. This may well turn out to be a smart thing!

Put your best foot forward

But only if your shoes are clean!
What I mean of course is make sure you continually present yourself in the best possible way.

Your appearance will make a huge difference as to how you are perceived. Especially in the workplace.

Correct spelling, being able to write grammatically and numerical ability are all extremely important. If you feel you need to brush up on any of these then take urgent steps to do so.

Punctuality and reliability are also going to have a positive impact. So pay attention to the way you conduct yourself.

Know who your real friends are.

People you are friends with today may well still be your friends many years from now. So be sure that they really are your friends!

Don't associate with people who will have a damaging affect on you. We are all susceptible to the influence of others....but never more so than when we are young. So ask yourself who is influencing you right now?

It's very important that the people you spend time with, and share your life, with are going to add to your well-being and not be destructive.

It's really sad to see some of the spiteful comments that some people post on Twitter and other social media platforms. Whether they are motivated by jealousy or a deep rooted hatred of others doing well I've no idea. But they can cause real distress to those who become the target of their nastiness. No doubt these disturbed individuals were bullies at school too.

Thankfully most people are decent and will want to see you do well. Surround yourself with people who care for you and who will be supportive.

Your environment will eventually dictate who and what you become.

If you need any further convincing go and visit a young offenders institute and find out from the inmates what kind of environment they were raised in.

The converse is also true of course.

Have fun today

Make the most of every day. That won't always be easy. You're bound to encounter some tough situations and difficulties from time to time. How you deal with them will depend largely upon your attitude. So, while you're still young, get into the habit of looking for the 'bright side' when faced with adversity.

Whatever may be bothering you today will almost certainly not seem nearly such a nightmare or catastrophe in hindsight.

I'm not so old that I can't remember the intensity of emotions that I experienced when I was in my late teens and early twenties. Things I can smile about now were almost a matter of 'life or death' to me at the time. Especially the first loves and early rejections! But in reality, as you'll discover, there is very little that doesn't eventually become less important or less painful. Take my word for it....the world isn't coming to an end!

Develop a happy disposition. Be a good person. Work hard at whatever you do.....that doesn't mean long hours, it means make the hours that you do work count.

Don't put things off. Especially don't put off having a great time while still young and independent.

If you get into the habit of living your life to the full it will be come the habit of a lifetime! The best thing you could possibly do.

So enjoy being who you are, what you are and where you are. Remember...Carpe Diem...seize the day.

But don't ignore tomorrow!

Look forward to tomorrow! It's just a day away. Every day has a tomorrow that's just a day away! And the good news is that most people find life gets better as they get older. You almost certainly will find that becomes true for you too.

As years go by, and you eventually leave your twenties, I'm confident that you'll have grown in confidence, developed some great relationships, made enduring friendships, gained lots of wisdom and learned to exercise good judgement. There's no rush.

The hardest thing when young is to imagine how life will be in years to come.

Things we take for granted today were inconceivable when I was in my twenties.

You'll be saying the same thing fifty years from now!

Smart phones and Tablets, Skype and FaceTime, Google, Facebook and Twitter, Kindles, SatNav and thousands of Apps for all kinds of things.

Even in our wildest dreams we could never have imagined what incredible things would be commonplace and in everyday use. At the beginning of my twenties we were still watching black and white TV and the word 'Internet' wasn't even in the dictionary!

It will be just as impossible to predict what will be taken for granted in the years to come. That's one of the many things that make life so exciting.

However there is one thing that I will predict. **Your future in forty or fifty years from now will be shaped by many of the things you do today.**

If I could urge you to do just one thing as a result of reading this book it would be to start the habit of saving ten per cent of everything you earn....beginning right now. Go back and read the two items under the headings Money and Wealth.

There is no way I can emphasise enough the importance to you of doing this.

I know it's almost impossible at your age to think in such a long term way. And I know there will be so many things you want to spend all your money on today and the next day etc. But trust me on this. If you would have the discipline to do this from today it will soon become habit. It won't be difficult a year from now. There will never be a better time for you to begin.

My generation......the so called 'baby boomers' have been incredibly fortunate. Many are retiring on generous pensions. Most have built substantial equity in their homes which they can release by moving to a smaller house. They have money to spend.

The first house I bought in the mid sixties was a newly built semi detached house near Maidstone in Kent. It cost £4,000. I see that it sold recently for £220,000 !

That's fifty-five times the original price! To put this into perspective the average annual income at that time was around £1,000. Today's average income is £25,000 a year but would have to be £55,000 if the same ratio applied.

History in terms of house price rises will not repeat itself in your lifetime. There is no way that house prices will rise at twice the rate of incomes over the next fifty years. House prices today are already so high that it's extremely difficult for first time buyers, so common sense tells us that they can't rise in the future at the same rate as they have in the past.

So don't count on your house, whenever you buy one, to make you rich.

I'm not trying to scare you........or perhaps maybe I am.

Now listen up.

The next generation of retirees, people currently in their forties and fifties are not going to be as fortunate as the generation that precedes them. They won't all have big pensions. Many may not even have a pension at all of any note. The value of future pensions based on investment results will not be anywhere near as generous as final salary schemes which are virtually a thing of the past.

The pensioners of tomorrow will have less equity in their homes too. Even today, most people retiring at sixty five will have exhausted their savings within seven years.

Since average life expectancy in the UK is currently eighty-four (longer in England and Wales) that leaves at least twelve very lean years after the nest egg is gone.

The problem is going to get worse as people continue to live longer.

I'm really sorry to feel the need to be telling you all this. After all, you're still young and shouldn't have to be burdened with these harsh realities. But the fact is, unless you were born to wealthy parents who will leave you a large inheritance, or able to give you a substantial leg up while they are still alive, you have to begin to act now.

I'm not suggesting you rush to buy into a pension. But I am urging you to start saving and investing and become financially savvy. You can't make money work for you until you have some!

Nobody knows what lies ahead in terms of how the world will continue to evolve. Governments will come and go. Economies will rise and fall. Changes will occur that are beyond our capability to second guess today. There will be conflicts and natural disasters in the future as there have been since time began.

But one thing I can tell you for sure. There's no fun in poverty. And there will be millions of people living on the breadline as people live longer, as they surely will.

Money isn't everything......but it brings freedom. And freedom is everything.

Let's end on a high note.

The world is your oyster....or so the saying goes! Stretching before you is an abundance of opportunity and a lifetime of adventure. I really believe that there has never been a better time to be alive than today.

Whatever the world is going to offer you, will be in direct proportion to what you will offer the world. So make every moment count.

Thank you so much for joining me on this journey.

May I wish you everything you wish for yourself.